D0466583

WORLD HISTORY

The Bombing of Pearl Harbor

By John F. Wukovits

LUCENT BOOKS
A part of Gale, Cengage Learning

GALE
CENGAGE Learning

Detroit • New York • San Francisco • New Haven, Conn • Waterville, Maine • London

LIBRARY OF CONGRESS CATALOGING-IN-PUBLICATION DATA

Wukovits, John F., 1944-
   The bombing of Pearl Harbor / by John F. Wukovits.
      p. cm. -- (World history)
   Includes bibliographical references and index.
   ISBN 978-1-4205-0330-2 (hardcover)
   1. Pearl Harbor (Hawaii), Attack on, 1941--Juvenile literature.
   2. World War, 1939-1945--Causes--Juvenile literature. I. Title.
   D767.92.W85 2011
   940.54'26693--dc22

                                                              2010035993

Lucent Books
27500 Drake Rd.
Farmington Hills, MI 48331

ISBN-13: 978-1-4205-0330-2
ISBN-10: 1-4205-0330-8

Printed in the United States of America
1 2 3 4 5 6 7 14 13 12 11 10

Printed by Bang Printing, Brainerd, MN, 1st Ptg., 02/2011

Contents

Foreword

Each year, on the first day of school, nearly every history teacher faces the task of explaining why his or her students should study history. Many reasons have been given. One is that lessons exist in the past from which contemporary society can benefit and learn. Another is that exploration of the past allows us to see the origins of our customs, ideas, and institutions. Concepts such as democracy, ethnic conflict, or even things as trivial as fashion or mores, have historical roots.

Reasons such as these impress few students, however. If anything, these explanations seem remote and dull to young minds. Yet history is anything but dull. And therein lies what is perhaps the most compelling reason for studying history: History is filled with great stories. The classic themes of literature and drama—love and sacrifice, hatred and revenge, injustice and betrayal, adversity and overcoming adversity – fill the pages of history books, feeding the imagination as well as any of the great works of fiction do.

The story of the Children's Crusade, for example, is one of the most tragic in history. In 1212 Crusader fever hit Europe. A call went out to the pope that all good Christians should journey to Jerusalem to drive out the hated Muslims and return the city to Christian control. Heeding the call, thousands of children made the journey. Parents bravely allowed many children to go, and entire communities were inspired by the faith of these small Crusaders. Unfortunately, many boarded ships captained by slave traders, who enthusiastically sold the children into slavery as soon as they arrived at their destination. Thousands died from disease, exposure, and starvation on the long march across Europe to the Mediterranean Sea. Others perished at sea.

Another story, from a modern and more familiar place, offers a soul-wrenching view of personal humiliation but also the ability to rise above it. Hatsuye Egami was one of 110,000 Japanese Americans sent to internment camps during World War II. "Since yesterday we Japanese have ceased to be human beings," he wrote in his diary. "We are numbers. We are no longer Egamis, but the number 23324. A tag with that number is on every trunk, suitcase and bag. Tags, also, on our breasts." Despite such dehumanizing treatment, most internees worked hard to control their bitterness. They created workable communities inside the camps and demonstrated again and again their loyalty as Americans.

These are but two of the many stories from history that can be found in the pages of the Lucent Books World History series. All World History titles rely on sound research and verifiable evidence, and all give students a clear sense of time, place, and chronology through maps and time-lines as well as text.

All titles include a wide range of authoritative perspectives that demonstrate the complexity of historical interpretation and sharpen the reader's critical thinking skills. Formally documented quotations and annotated bibliographies enable students to locate and evaluate sources, often instantaneously via the Internet, and serve as valuable tools for further research and debate.

Finally, Lucent's World History titles present rousing good stories, featuring vivid primary source quotations drawn from unique, sometimes obscure sources such as diaries, public records, and contemporary chronicles. In this way, the voices of participants and witnesses as well as important biographers and historians bring the study of history to life. As we are caught up in the lives of others, we are reminded that we too are characters in the ongoing human saga, and we are better prepared for our own roles.

Important Dates at the Time of

1918
World War I fighting ends after Allied and Central Powers sign armistice

August 18, 1920
Nineteenth Amendment gives women right to vote

October 28, 1922
Benito Mussolini comes to power in Italy

September 30, 1927
Babe Ruth sets home run record by hitting his sixtieth home run

1918

1923

1928

June 18, 1919
Treaty of Versailles is signed

May 3, 1926
U.S. Marines sent to occupy Nicaragua

October 192*
Stock market crash on Wall Street in New York Cit*
sends U.S. int*
Great Depress*

June 5, 1926
Chiang Kai-shek begins to gather power in China

November 4, 1922
Tomb of King Tut discovered in Egypt by Howard Carter

October 6, 1927
first talking movie, *The Jazz Singer*, opens

the Pearl Harbor Attack

September 19, 1931
Japan invades Manchuria

July 17, 1936
Spanish Civil War begins

August 5, 1936
Jesse Owens wins gold medal at the Berlin Olympics

January 30, 1933
Adolf Hitler becomes chancellor of Germany

July 7, 1937
Japan invades China

December 12, 1937
Japan sinks the U.S. gunboat *Panay*

September 1, 1939
Germany invades Poland and begins World War II

December 7, 1941
Japan attacks Pearl Harbor; United States enters World War II

1933　　　　　　　　　**1938**　　　　　　　　　**1943**

March 5, 1933
Franklin D. Roosevelt becomes U.S. president and launches New Deal

1934
Parker Brothers begins selling the game Monopoly

1934–1935
Mao Zedong sets out on the Long March in China

March 13, 1938
Hitler takes over Austria and makes it part of Germany

November 11, 1938
Nazis destroy Jewish homes and businesses in Germany

Surprise Attack

The USS *Tangier*, a seaplane tender (a ship that repairs, or tends to, other vessels), floated at its dock that peaceful Sunday morning at Pearl Harbor, Hawaii, the U.S. Navy's most important naval base in the Pacific Ocean. An occasional bird glided above while a gentle breeze caressed the ship. Nearby, the battleship *Utah* and the light cruisers the *Raleigh* and the *Detroit* lined the shore, while across the way, on the eastern side of Ford Island, seven battleships rested in splendid majesty, forming such an impressive array of power that sailors had dubbed it Battleship Row. To the servicepeople stationed there, it looked like December 7 would be another calm weekend day in Pearl Harbor, a Sunday filled with light duties aboard ships followed by visits to Hawaii's beaches and tourist attractions.

Lieutenant Richard L. Fruin had just gone out to the deck of the *Tangier* when he spotted a group of aircraft heading toward Ford Island. One week earlier, superiors had punished a navy pilot for flying in unauthorized areas, so Fruin assumed that some young flyer was in for a rough meeting with his commander when he landed. His thoughts abruptly halted when the planes passed overhead, with their red circles—representations of the rising sun, the Japanese war symbol—clearly visible. The planes swiftly dropped a string of bombs on Ford Island. The *Tangier*'s captain, Commander Clifton A.F. Sprague, bolted from his quarters and dashed to the bridge. "Quarters! Quarters!" he shouted into the speaker system. "Hurry!"[1]

On the eastern end of Ford Island, the ship's band had just begun playing "The Star-Spangled Banner" aboard the battleship *Nevada* when the Japanese planes let fall a stream of bombs. The band bravely played on through the attack's opening moments and finished the tune, then raced for their battle stations.

Japan's surprise attack on Pearl Harbor on December 7, 1941, brought the United States into World War II.

Like thousands of others at Pearl Harbor that morning, Lieutenant Fruin and the band of the *Nevada* had just witnessed the opening moments of their nation's involvement in World War II. The Japanese, with whom the United States had been at political odds for years, had unleashed a surprise air attack directly against the heart of American power in the Pacific—its vast naval base at Pearl Harbor on the island of Oahu, Hawaii. Within a few hours much of America's military arsenal, and its first line of defense, rested on Pearl Harbor's bottom, leaving the nation and its military in shock, scrambling for a response to the numbing attack. December 7, 1941, proved to be one of those moments in history when nothing afterward seemed the same as before, a day that profoundly changed peoples' lives and nations' futures.

Chapter One

Opening Act of World War II

Though the United States' involvement in the fighting phase of World War II did not begin until December 1941, events that had taken place long before that date had resulted in Lieutenant Fruin and his comrades' fighting for their lives at Pearl Harbor. The origins of World War II had appeared at the end of the conflict that had preceded it—World War I.

The Treaty of Versailles

On June 28, 1919, representatives of twenty-seven nations gathered at Versailles, France, to sign the peace treaty to formally end World War I. Four long years of destructive strife, from 1914 to 1918, had wearied the Allied nations of the United States, England, France, Belgium, and Italy in their struggle against Germany and its allies. They, as well as the other nations involved in the conflict, mourned the loss of millions of young men.

Though war was over, the hope for a brighter future was often overshadowed by the Allied nations' desire to seek revenge on Germany for starting four cruel years of war. Their armed forces, people, and economies had suffered horribly, and they intended to make Germany pay for all the harm it had caused. Though the Treaty of Versailles marked an end to World War I—a war that American president Woodrow Wilson called the "war to end all wars"—most historians agree that the harsh peace treaty enraged Germans and sowed the seeds for future conflict.

"Germany howled," wrote historian Charles Bracelen Flood of Germany in 1920. "Nine months earlier, when the German public had first learned what the treaty would impose, the anger had been tempered with a measure of shock and fear, but the Germany of 1920 reacted with a fighting attitude born of desperation. In the past months Germans had seen what all those treaty terms really meant."[2]

The Treaty of Versailles set the terms for the end of World War I and created harsh conditions that provided impetus for a new war.

In creating the terms of the treaty, the Allied nations' first order of business was to take apart the German war machine and so weaken Germany that the nation could no longer pose a threat. The 440 terms that composed the Treaty of Versailles placed immense financial and military debts on defeated Germany and its allies. Germany was required to admit guilt for causing the war, pay $100 billion to repair the damage it had done, and reduce its military to a pitiful one hundred thousand men. The nation had to hand over much land that had been formerly under its control, including possessions in the Pacific.

With such severe terms imposed on Germany, the Treaty of Versailles practically guaranteed that another war would erupt in the near future. German citizens disliked any mention of the hated treaty, and the situation was ripe for a talented leader to unite people inside Germany and create problems in nations along its borders.

At the same time, the United States, which had emerged from World War I as the next superpower, intended never again to become involved in a European conflict. Feeling safe behind two immense oceans that shielded them from both European and Asian aggressors, the American people resisted involvement in problems abroad, and a period of isolationism, or staying out of others' problems, dominated American policy.

"We never appreciated so keenly as now the foresight exercised by our forefathers in emigrating [moving away] from Europe,"[3] wrote one Indiana newspaper editor. While Europe and Asia faced increasing international problems, the United States shunned world events and focused on matters inside its own borders as much as possible.

Challenges to World Peace

The Treaty of Versailles was barely in place before two men who would soon threaten the new peace began their rise to power: Benito Mussolini in Italy and Adolf Hitler in Germany. Unsettled conditions greeted Mussolini when he returned from duty in the war. Unemployment was widespread, and fellow citizens were angry and upset that the Treaty of Versailles had not included more favorable terms for Italy. Using stirring speeches and clever organizational skills over the next few years, Mussolini gradually gained the support of many of his fellow citizens. Quickly sensing an opportunity to gather together a following with his black-shirted *fasci di combattimento* (combat groups), Mussolini swept into power with his Fascist Party, first as a member of the Italian Parliament (congress) in 1921, and then as the nation's leader the next year.

Mussolini enacted speedy reforms in government and industry before signing a 1925 decree making him dictator. Among his most cherished goals was to return Italy to a place of glory, a renown it had not commanded since the days of the Roman Empire almost two thousand years earlier.

At almost the same time Mussolini came to power in Italy, Adolf Hitler and his Nazi Party were gaining popularity in Germany. A powerful speaker who moved crowds with his fiery speech and hypnotic eyes, Hitler encouraged pride in the nation as well as anti-Semitism—hatred directed at the country's Jews. These popular stands served to enlarge the party ranks. Germans flocked to the new party, drawn by Hitler's promises of a better Germany and, for many, by their own anti-Semitic sentiments.

An American reporter stationed in Berlin, William Shirer, watched Hitler work his magic before a spellbound audience. "Hitler began with a long harangue which he has often given before, but never tires of repeating, about the injustices of the Versailles Treaty and the peacefulness of Germans,"[4] Shirer noted. Shirer also noticed that many listeners rose to their feet and shouted their approval of what they heard. Hitler adopted the swastika, or armed cross, as a party symbol for his National Socialist German Workers' Party, called the Nazi Party after a shortened form of the first word. By 1923 the party's ranks had multiplied from 1,000 to 150,000.

The October 1929 stock market crash on Wall Street, the business sector in New York City, and the resulting Great Depression spun industrialized nations into an economic collapse. In speech after speech, Hitler promised that he and the Nazi Party would bring jobs to the vast numbers of unemployed people and return glory and honor to Germany.

The Rise of Benito Mussolini

The future Italian dictator was born in Predappio, Italy, on July 29, 1883. The youthful Benito Mussolini was so hard to handle that his mother sent him to a strict Catholic school, from which he was promptly expelled for stabbing another student.

By 1909 the flamboyant young man had become involved in Italian Socialist Party politics. He edited a weekly newspaper called *La Lotta di Classe (The Class Struggle)* and spent minor stints in jail for his rabid antigovernment views.

When World War I threw his country into turmoil, Mussolini changed his political opinions and became an ardent supporter of the war effort. He started a second newspaper, *Il Popolo d'Italia (The People of Italy)* that encouraged citizens to join in the war effort, then entered the army. He served for seventeen months and was wounded in a grenade accident in 1917.

Mussolini returned to a fragmented Italy. Widespread unemployment placed many families in danger of losing their homes, and anger that the Treaty of Versailles had not included more favorable terms for Italy produced cries for a remedy. Quickly sensing an opportunity to consolidate a following, Mussolini organized a March 23, 1919, meeting in Milan. With almost 150 in attendance, Mussolini formed the black-shirted *Fasci di Combattimento* (Combat Squads) and declared that his new political party would support better treatment of former soldiers and a stronger government.

Rallying behind the slogan "Believe, obey, fight," Mussolini and his followers quickly expanded. Many Italians were discontented with poor government and angry about labor strikes that disrupted the economy. Their frustration made them receptive to Mussolini's message.

With such broad support, Mussolini won a seat in Parliament in 1921. While his Combat Squads terrorized opponents into silence, Mussolini continued to increase his power. On October 29, 1922, in hopes of quelling the nationwide discontent, Italian king Victor Emmanuel summoned Mussolini to Rome and asked him to form a government.

Mussolini enacted speedy reforms in government and industry before signing a 1925 decree making him dictator. He fired thirty-five thousand civil servants, forced teachers to sign oaths of loyalty, and ordered that newspaper reporters had to be approved by the party.

The rest of the world, caught up in its own problems, turned a blind eye to these events.

The Rise of Adolf Hitler

A dolf Hitler was born on April 20, 1889, in the small Austrian town of Braunau-am-Inn. The fourth child of Klara and Alois Hitler, Hitler experienced a troubled early life. He dropped out of school at the age of sixteen to pursue his love of art, but his hopes were crushed when he twice failed the entrance examination for admission to the prestigious Vienna Arts Academy.

Though he occasionally collected money by painting postcards and small watercolors, Hitler had no real means of support in the Austrian capital. The hungry youth roamed the streets as a homeless vagabond, begged for his food, and sometimes slept in poorhouses for men. While in Vienna he read the anti-Semitic (Jew-hating) writings of various German thinkers as well as the views of those who advocated a strong German state.

World War I saved Hitler. Instead of remaining destitute, he enrolled in the German army where he served with distinction, delivering messages from commanding officers in the rear to soldiers fighting on the front lines. For courage under fire, Hitler was twice decorated by his superiors.

On October 13, 1918, Hitler was exposed to deadly chlorine gas that left him blind and gasping for breath. He eventually recovered, but before he could return to the front Germany signed a treaty of surrender to end the war. Upset at the war's termination, Hitler claimed that politicians back home who should have continued the fight betrayed Germany's brave soldiers.

Hitler's consternation did not diminish when he returned to Germany, where he encountered increasing German resentment toward the catastrophic terms of the Treaty of Versailles. For a time Hitler remained in the army and served as a spy to uncover dissident political factions.

He became enamored with one of the groups he investigated, the German Workers' Party, which he joined in September 1919 as member number seven. Within two years he had resigned from the army and risen to the head of the party. Hitler, feasting upon the people's dissatisfaction with the government and a long-standing animosity toward Jews, was determined to create an organization that would rectify the current predicament.

Adolf Hitler played on the German people's dissatisfaction with their harsh conditions after World War I and sentiment against Jews to rise to power.

Hitler increased his power in 1932 when his Nazis captured more than one-third of the national vote and became the leading party in Germany. On January 30, 1933, Hitler was named chancellor, the nation's second-highest position. In March of that year the German Reichstag, or legislature, passed laws that made Germany a virtual dictatorship led by Hitler and the Nazis.

Aggressive Moves

Now that the two major opponents to world peace were firmly in place in Germany and Italy, they began to inch toward open warfare. Hitler sensed that opposition from democratic countries, still weary from the death and destruction caused by World War I, would be feeble. With minor support from Mussolini, he boldly ignored the Treaty of Versailles. He understood that England and France shuddered at the thought of war and would do almost anything to avoid it. This plan of avoiding conflict, called appeasement, dominated French and British policy for much of the decade.

The two dictators wasted little time enlarging their power. In 1935 Mussolini invaded the African nation of Ethiopia. Haile Selassie, Ethiopia's ruler, pleaded for aid from the League of Nations, an international organization formed to ensure world peace after World War I, but his words produced only weak penalties against Italy. Neither Britain nor France wanted war, so Mussolini was given a free hand to conquer the African country. Neither was Britain and France's failure to take firm action lost on Adolf Hitler.

Now that he had seen Great Britain and France shy away from employing force to halt Mussolini's demands, Hitler turned his gaze toward Austria, the home of 7 million citizens of German descent. Hitler used people friendly to Nazis inside Austria to stir up trouble and create a desire for German help in keeping peace inside the country. In early March 1938 he demanded that Nazis be placed in key government positions. When Austrian chancellor Kurt von Schusnigg refused, the German Army on March 12 poured across the Austrian border. Two days later, Hitler entered Vienna in triumph and announced the *Anschluss*—the union of Germany and Austria.

A joyful Hitler waited for any reaction from the democracies, and when none came he turned to the next nation on his list—Czechoslovakia, a country rich in natural resources and industry, and the possessor of a respected military. Czechoslovakia was home to 3 million Germans, mostly in the area called the Sudetenland along the western border. Hitler encouraged these people to demand that the Czechoslovakian government establish greater ties with Germany.

Since neither Britain nor France felt militarily strong enough to halt Hitler, their leaders pressured Czechoslovakian president Eduard Benes to yield to Hitler's demands. When Hitler threatened war if his mandates were not met, British prime minister Neville Chamberlain flew to Germany to assure him that he would arrange a peaceful transfer of the Sudetenland. On September 30, 1938, in an agreement signed at Munich, Hitler received the Sudetenland, leading Chamberlain to gush, "I believe it is peace in our time."[5] Time and events would prove how wrong that statement was.

According to some historians, had the democracies maintained a firm position and refused to hand over the Sudetenland, Hitler might have stopped making demands. As it was, Hitler's prestige never stood higher than after the Munich agreement. From thousands of miles away, Japan watched the developments with keen interest, as that nation's leaders had their own plans for expansion.

Within six months of Munich, Hitler devoured the rest of Czechoslovakia. On March 11, 1939, he ordered the pro-German party in the remainder of Czechoslovakia to announce their breaking away from that nation and to ask for Hitler's help. Four days later, German troops entered the capital city of Prague, and Czechoslovakia no longer existed.

Hitler's conquest of Czechoslovakia finally awakened the sleeping democracies. On March 17 Chamberlain declared that England, in conjunction with France, would oppose any further moves attempted by Hitler.

The United States Shuns Europe

While events in Europe moved inevitably toward war, the mightiest democracy in the world withdrew into its own

---

Hitler Hysteria

Newspaper correspondent William L. Shirer observed events in Germany in the 1930s as Hitler rose to power. In 1941 he published his account of those times, *Berlin Diary*. A phenomenon to which he repeatedly referred was the hold Hitler had on the German people, something akin to a movie star today. The quote below is from his entry for September 4, 1934.

About ten o'clock tonight I got caught in a mob of ten thousand hysterics who jammed the moat in front of Hitler's hotel, shouting: 'We want our Fuhrer [leader].' I was a little shocked at the faces, especially those of the women, when Hitler finally appeared on the balcony for a moment. They looked up at him as if he were a Messiah [savior], their faces transformed into something positively inhuman. If he had remained in sight for more than a few moments, I think many of the women would have swooned from excitement.

William L. Shirer. *Berlin Diary*. New York: Knopf, 1941, pp. 17–18.

U.S. president Franklin Roosevelt supported Great Britain and France against Hitler, but he lacked public and political support to involve the country in the conflict.

borders. Weary of intervening in Europe's affairs, the United States preferred to stay behind its gigantic barriers—the Atlantic Ocean on the European side and the Pacific Ocean on the Asian side. Secure behind the watery borders, the majority of American people focused on solving domestic problems, particularly ending the Great Depression, and left Europe to handle its own issues.

The spirit of isolationism carried into Congress, which enacted a series of laws, the Neutrality Acts, that made sure America would not take sides. Should war erupt, Congress forbade the shipment of weapons to warring nations and banned loans to warring countries.

The sorry state of the American military emboldened Hitler in Europe and an ever-watchful Japan in the Pacific. The once-mighty war machine that helped defeat Germany in World War I had plunged to less than 150,000 soldiers, ranking it no higher than eighteenth among world nations in 1940, behind Belgium, the Netherlands, and Portugal. Its navy and air forces fared no better. Even if the nation wanted to help, it could do little until its military modernized and expanded.

Great Britain and France possessed one powerful ally inside the United States—President Franklin D. Roosevelt. Far before most Americans, he saw the need to stand up to Hitler and tried to warn his nation about the threat of fascism, but he could do little without support from his fellow citizens and Congress. In the face of such potent opposition from the isolationists, Roosevelt had to adopt a cautious approach and hope that his nation would eventually see the wisdom of his arguments.

Poland Falls

With Czechoslovakia firmly in his grasp, Hitler turned his attention to Poland. As part of the price for losing World War I, Germany had been forced to yield the city of Danzig and the Polish Corridor—a wide strip of land through German territory that connected Poland to the Baltic Sea. Hitler was determined to get back that territory, which not only was the largest portion of German land taken but also separated Germany into two parts. In his quest to regain the territory, Hitler found a willing partner in the leader of the Soviet Union. Joseph Stalin was upset that England and France had refused to assist Czechoslovakia, and he felt slighted that he had not been asked to take part in the Munich talks.

In exchange for a promise that the Soviet Union would not take part in war should Germany attack Poland, Hitler agreed to hand Stalin much of eastern Poland and the nations of Latvia, Lithuania, and Estonia. The pact, signed on August 23, 1939, gave Hitler a free hand to attack Poland. Should the French and British military assemble in the west, Hitler could focus an overwhelming amount of military might against those nations without concern about defending against an attack from Stalin in the east.

Announcement of the Nazi-Soviet Nonaggression Pact stunned England and France. The Allies realized all too late that military might, not appeasement, was needed to halt the German dictator. The French government, which had promised aid to Poland as early as 1936, started getting its troops ready for war. In Great Britain, Chamberlain enacted a series of steps—he signed an agreement with Poland to provide military assistance should it be attacked, canceled leaves for all British troops, and brought Winston Churchill, a politician who had served as First Lord of the Admiralty (head of the navy) in World War I, back into the government to once again fulfill that post.

War Begins

On August 31, 1939, a group of German soldiers wearing Polish uniforms crept across the German-Polish border into the small town of Gleiwitz and seized the radio transmitter. Acting as Polish undercover agents, the German troops broadcast a message urging all Poles to attack Germany. The Germans had brought with them several inmates from Dachau, the first German concentration camp, which had been opened by the Nazis in 1933. The Germans dressed the inmates in Polish uniforms and then machine-gunned them down. Their bodies were

German forces practiced blitzkrieg, a destructive pattern of air attack. Warsaw, Poland, experienced such an attack in 1939.

strewn about the area to make it appear that a Polish invasion of Germany had begun.

Hitler used this "incident" to hurl his mighty army at the confused Poles. On September 1 the German army crossed into Poland. When Great Britain and France declared war on Germany two days later, World War II was on in earnest.

What the German forces achieved in the next four weeks fascinated and frightened the rest of the world. They struck with breathtaking speed. The pattern, called *blitzkrieg*, or lightning warfare, was the same along both the northern and southern borders. German aircraft attacked targets ahead of advancing German tanks to destroy airfields and communications, instill fear, and force Polish civilians to flee their homes and flood the roads, thereby blocking the likely retreat route for the Polish army. Dive-bombers plunged in an almost-vertical dive toward refugees.

Tanks followed on the heels of the aircraft, ignoring concentrations of Polish soldiers to reach the rear areas, where they attacked command centers and communications areas. German infantry then moved forward, destroyed pockets of resistance, and headed on to the next center of opposition. In some areas German armored units advanced 25 miles (40km) in the initial day against surprised Polish defenders. Hitler's stunning operation dismantled the Polish army in four weeks.

Two days after the attacks started, Great Britain and France declared war on Germany. The two democracies, though, did little to assist the Poles, who bravely battled their German foe. Some historians contend that both nations missed a perfect opportunity to halt World War II in its tracks. A determined drive might have succeeded in crashing through weak German defenses along the border and proceeded to threaten some of Germany's famed industrial centers.

The reality, though, was that at this time the democratic nations lacked the desire and resources to fight a major conflict. Neither France nor England wanted war, and both hoped that once Hitler finished with Poland, his land lust would be satisfied. Memories of the ghastly losses of World War I produced inaction on the part of the democracies, including the United States, another meek response that was not lost on interested leaders in Japan. "We must not push Japan too much at this time"[6] cautioned U.S. secretary of state Cordell Hull.

Hitler was clearly not finished with his invasions in Europe after taking Poland. To ensure access to valuable Scandinavian iron ore, and to have more airfields and U-boat (submarine) bases on the Atlantic coast, he sent German troops into Norway on April 9, 1940. German soldiers rushed ashore near Trondheim, Narvik, and other locations along Norway's coast against light opposition. In May, Germany advanced into the Netherlands, Belgium, and Luxembourg. The German army entered French borders on May 12.

The Fall of France

The German military machine posted its greatest achievement with the speedy destruction of the British and French armies (known as the Allies) in France. The opposing armies fielded equal numbers. The difference lay in the equipment and planning. The Allies positioned a thousand more tanks along the border than Germany had, but they spread them out along the length of the French border while Germany put most of its tanks in one location. While German soldiers enjoyed the newest and best weapons, England and France relied on outdated equipment.

The Germans had also mastered the use of air and land forces. The invasion of Poland illustrated the importance of using the two arms together. Their military triumphs, based on a combination of thoroughly prepared, disciplined troops and a clever, new plan for their use, provided a model for Japanese leaders. If bold action and the willingness to take risks worked in Europe, it could also work in the Pacific.

The Germans advanced on an undefended Paris on June 14, 1940, and on June 21 the fighting in France ended when the French government surrendered to the German invaders. Hitler now turned his attention to Great Britain.

President Roosevelt ordered his military to gather any extra items that could be spared for delivery to a besieged England, and soon a stream of supplies headed across the Atlantic. Bolstered by American aid, and shortly by their entry into the war, England grew stronger and became

Hitler and his men walk away from the Eiffel Tower in Paris. German troops quickly captured France and its undefended capital in 1940.

the platform from which the Allied Forces would eventually defeat Hitler.

Reaction to the War in the United States

While war raged in Europe, a different battle split the United States into two camps. Isolationists, led by the America First Committee, favored retreating behind the protection of the oceans and ignoring European matters. Interventionists, guided by the Committee to Defend America by Aiding the Allies, believed that the nation best protected itself by helping other nations stop Hitler. During the mid-1930s the isolationist camp had boasted more supporters and was able to convince Congress to pass the Neutrality Acts.

Roosevelt, who had long understood that the nation would soon be caught up in the war, took advantage of the shift in public feeling by asking Congress to change the Neutrality Acts so the United States could sell arms to warring nations. Congress agreed, as long as the purchasing countries paid cash for the material and transported it in their own ships. This "cash and carry" program, though outwardly neutral in application, heavily favored the Allies because the powerful British navy, not Germany's, controlled the seas.

Roosevelt also requested more funds to strengthen the defense of the Panama Canal, the vital route taken by each American warship traveling from the Atlantic Ocean to the Pacific, but Congress and the American people swung to his support in large numbers only after Hitler swept through France and other European countries in the spring of 1940. Roosevelt and his military advisers watched Hitler's 136 divisions push across France, and then compared that powerful force with their own United States Army of five divisions. Something had to be done quickly to offset that unbalance.

In a May 16, 1940, speech Roosevelt asked for the money to train five hundred thousand men and build more weapons. He stunned the nation by setting a goal of building fifty thousand aircraft per year, an unthinkable number to many experts, but the crafty politician knew that the American public loved a challenge and responded to nice, round numbers.

Congress passed the National Defense Tax Bill in June 1940 to fund the military buildup and authorized Roosevelt to construct a navy large enough to successfully counter threats in both the Atlantic and Pacific oceans. Later that year the Selective Training and Service Act required every male between the ages of twenty-one and thirty-six to register for a draft. Shortly, more than 1 million men would be drafted into the armed forces.

Roosevelt took a more aggressive action in September when he gave England fifty aging United States destroyers in exchange for naval and air bases in the Western Hemisphere. Churchill's navy desperately needed destroyers to protect shipping and shield England from the Germans, and though he received opposition from politicians and navy officials, he and Roosevelt closed the deal. The first eight destroyers were handed over on September 9 as the British were mounting their heroic stand in the Battle of Britain (July 10 to October 31), in which they beat off the Germans over the English Channel and the southern and eastern coasts of England in a desperate bombing campaign.

Most Americans now agreed with their president, but Roosevelt's words, effective as they were, could not match the impact of the glorious display presented by the German army in its steady march to the sea in France. Each time a German Panzer (tank) unit cut a wide path through French and British soldiers, American isolationism lost support. Each time Germany organized a bombing raid across the channel to England, more people swung toward the interventionist side.

Roosevelt's most clever manner of helping Churchill came in late 1940 with the program known as Lend-Lease. If a neighbor's home was on fire and he needed your hose, he told his fellow Americans, no one would first charge the neighbor for the hose. Instead, he would loan him the hose and expect it back later. Lend-Lease was meant to work that way, said Roosevelt. The United States would lend England the equipment it needed now, and not worry about payment until after the crisis was over. The next week Roosevelt added that to stop Hitler from controlling all of Europe, America had to become the "arsenal of democracy." The country's factories had to turn out tanks, planes, and rifles in large measure, while other democracies used the weapons to battle the dictators. The shrewd president figured that his fellow citizens would support Lend-Lease. He believed they saw Hitler as a real evil and would view Lend-Lease as an acceptable alternative to open warfare.

As events in Europe continued to draw Roosevelt's attention, the Japanese had set out on a program designed to strengthen its control in Asia and the western Pacific. That country's leaders understood that, sooner or later, the bold steps might lead to conflict with the United States, which had interests in that region. If Japan were to have any chance of weakening that powerful adversary, its military would have to devise a unique action, a surprise that would knock the United States on its heels.

Chapter Two

The United States Moves Toward War

While Hitler threatened world peace in Europe, Japan and the United States moved from an uneasy peace to the brink of open warfare in the Pacific. Though President Roosevelt actively involved the nation in European affairs in an attempt to aid Churchill's besieged Britain, it would be events on the other side of the world that would sweep the United States into the war.

The United States in the Pacific

Sources of friction between Japan and the United States existed long before war actually touched their borders in 1941. As early as the late 1800s, American politicians proclaimed that it was the nation's "manifest destiny" to expand beyond its continental borders into the Pacific. They viewed with lusty eyes the profitable natural resources in Asia and intended to set up and maintain businesses in the region. American manufacturers, eager to possess a ready market for the vast amount of goods their factories turned out, lent their support.

Following the successful conclusion of the war with Spain in 1898, the United States received possession of the Philippine Islands. Standing 1,400 miles (2,240km) southwest of Japan, the Philippines offered plentiful natural resources, such as oil and rubber, as well as excellent sites for military bases. The United States sent soldiers to occupy the subjected nation, thereby conveying the message to Japan, which also sought to expand throughout Asia, that the United States, and not Japan, would be master in the Pacific.

The United States did not stand as the only outside power in the area. For more than three centuries European nations had seized and colonized nations on the Asian mainland and islands in the Pacific. France controlled Indochina; Germany held different island groups in the Pacific;

Artist John Gast painted an image of the U.S. belief in "manifest destiny," the idea that the United States should expand beyond its current borders. This belief helped spur U.S. involvement in the Pacific region.

the Netherlands occupied oil-rich Java and portions of the East Indies; Great Britain held the mighty fortress at Singapore as well as Burma and India.

Every western nation subjected the native populations to economic and political control and considered them as little more than children to be governed. Europeans living among the native groups acted superior to the darker-skinned residents and greedily gobbled up land and products throughout the Pacific. One official in the Dutch East Indies proudly boasted that the Netherlands had been in power in Asia for three hundred years, and that they would remain there for another three hundred years.

In December 1907, President Theodore Roosevelt increased the American presence in the Pacific by ordering the United States Navy to steam through the region. In doing so, he sent a message to Japan that the United States intended to defend its Pacific interests, especially the Philippines. Unfortunately for Roosevelt, once the navy left Pacific waters, he had no military tool with which to stop any aggressive Japanese moves. Congress

The Rise of Franklin D. Roosevelt

Franklin Delano Roosevelt was born on January 30, 1882, in New York to an affluent family. The intelligent, athletic youth sailed through school with ease and entered Harvard University in 1900. While there he fell in love with his fifth cousin once removed, Eleanor Roosevelt, and married her in 1905.

Roosevelt embarked on a political career that eventually placed him in the White House during America's darkest hours since the Civil War. After serving as a New York state senator, he accepted the post of assistant secretary of the navy in 1913, then gained stature among the Democratic Party until he was named the party's vice presidential candidate in 1920.

His career seemed over in 1921 when he was stricken with polio and became paralyzed from the waist down. With an indomitable spirit, Roosevelt returned from his illness to be elected governor of New York in 1928. Four years later the American people turned to him to solve the problems of the Great Depression by voting him in as president of the country.

In the White House, Roosevelt instituted a group of social programs, called the New Deal, that gave hope to the American public that the government could help remedy economic ills. His famous "Fireside Chats," delivered over radio to a worried nation, inspired the American people and made them believe that better times awaited.

did not want to start an expensive arms race and so did not approve the money needed to add ships that could be stationed in the area. Until the time came when the country had built enough ships to keep a force permanently stationed in East Asia, United States policy in the Pacific existed without the means to enforce it.

Japan in the Pacific

Japan's role in the Pacific and East Asia was more complex than that of the United States. In the eyes of many Japanese, a leading position in the region guaranteed the nation's survival, while to accept an inferior status would send it to the backwaters of world rankings.

Unlike the United States, which enjoyed spacious land into which its population could spread, Japan existed inside a tiny area framed by water. The more the nation's population increased, the less space became available. Approximately 80 million people lived in Japan in the 1920s, whose total area equaled that of the state of Montana—except that Montana had a population of less than 1 million. If Japan, the most crowded nation on earth, were to grow,

A Japanese envoy walks with French officials in French Indo-China. Japan sought to extend its influence in the Pacific region, believing that a strong presence was key to the nation's survival.

it had to acquire land beyond its borders. When Japanese expansionists studied the nearby areas, most eyes turned west toward the Asian mainland and China.

As an island nation, Japan had to import much of its raw materials and food products. Japan's people could grow only a certain amount of their national needs, and to fill the rest the nation's leaders had to look elsewhere. Almost 70 percent of the country's supply of zinc and tin, 90 percent of its lead, and all of its cotton,

wool, aluminum, and rubber had to be imported from other countries.

When they sought raw materials from Asia, Japanese leaders crashed head-on into European interests. The country needed rubber, tin, and bauxite (aluminum ore) from Burma and Malaya, but those nations were controlled by Great Britain. Indochina's vast rubber plantations contained valuable material, but France held sway in that country. The most desired product, oil, stood in plentiful amounts in the East Indies, but the

Dutch maintained a stranglehold on the region. Everywhere Japan turned, a European nation appeared to block the path to its future.

To provide stability in its own land, Japan believed it had to control the Pacific and Asian mainland. Japanese leaders masked their intentions by proclaiming that, as the only Asian nation to rise to the status of world power, Japan, not European nations or the United States, had an inherent right to rule in the region. This attitude placed Japan in direct opposition to similar interests expressed by the United States.

Japanese activity in the Pacific alarmed politicians and military officials in the United States. Since they were used to referring to East Asians as the "yellow peril," a threat to the white-dominated rule that had existed in the Pacific and throughout the world, many American leaders distrusted the Japanese. Japan's desire to expand beyond its borders just made this attitude stronger.

Peace and Friction in the 1920s

The decade of the 1920s saw an escalation of harsh feelings between the United States and Japan. Though built on the principles of equality and fair play, the United States government had a shameful history of bigotry toward Japanese and Americans of Japanese descent. In 1907 the school board in San Francisco, California, had refused to allow Japanese children to attend school. Six years later the California state legislature passed a law prohibiting Japanese from owning land, and in 1924 Congress passed a law that banned the immigration of Asians. Japan was so enraged by this 1924 law that on the day it took effect in the United States, the Japanese government declared a national day of dishonor.

People in Japan, especially younger, more radical army officers, were angry at what they viewed as unfair treatment from foreign governments and looked to their military to correct the situation. For a time Japanese militants who urged expansion onto the Asian mainland were held in check by more moderate forces, but world events turned feelings in Japan toward the militants. Military extremists criticized moderates for giving away too much military might in the 1920s peace accords and called for a new policy that would emphasize conquest and expansion.

From early 1936 on, militarists gained more influence. An alarmed American ambassador to Japan, Joseph Grew, warned Washington that the Japanese militarists grew more powerful every day and that they intended to expand into China and other areas of the Pacific.

First Thrusts: Manchuria and China

The first violent act that led to World War II in the Pacific occurred on September 18, 1931, when a bomb exploded along the Japanese-controlled South Manchuria Railway near Mukden, Manchuria. Units of the Japanese army had been stationed in Korea since the Russo-Japanese War of 1904–1905 to protect Japanese interests. After the bombing, Japan immediately launched an invasion to overrun all of

Japanese soldiers bury Chinese prisoners alive outside of Nanking. Japan's extreme actions in China strained its relations with the United States.

Manchuria, which they quickly seized and renamed Manchukuo.

Other nations, including the United States, condemned the invasion. When the League of Nations refused to recognize the state of Manchukuo, Japan withdrew from the organization in 1933 and continued to use its new possession for its own benefit. Since many nations were in the midst of battling economic problems stemming from the 1929 Wall Street crash, they did not consider using military force to halt these aggressive moves.

Japan, as did Hitler and Mussolini in Europe, noticed this refusal to take action and embarked on a bolder course of action as the decade unfolded.

A more serious incident occurred on the Asian mainland on July 7, 1937, when Japanese soldiers opened fire on Chinese troops at the Marco Polo Bridge near Peking (today Beijing), China. It was never decided who had fired first, but the Japanese army used the incident as a reason to unleash a huge offensive against the Chinese.

The Japanese reacted swiftly and brutally to Chinese resistance. The worst bloodshed unfolded in December 1937 at Nanking, where Japanese troops killed more than two hundred thousand Chinese.

The United States protested these criminal acts against a nation with whom they shared close bonds, developed by American missionaries who had long worked in China. But since no nation was willing or able to mount military action to hold back the Japanese, the protest achieved nothing. The Japanese continued to plunder China at will.

The events in China pushed the United States and Japan further apart. The Japanese believed that the United States had no right to interfere in Asian matters, and the United States was shocked at the brutality with which the Japanese treated fellow Asians. More and more, the two viewed each other as bitter foes.

The *Panay* Incident

Relations between the United States and Japan worsened in December 1937 when Japanese aircraft attacked the U.S. gunboat *Panay*. The gunboat was removing the last of the American embassy staff from the besieged town of Nanking when a squadron of Japanese aircraft shelled the small boat. The American commander ordered everyone over the side of the burning craft into lifeboats, which sought the shelter of high reeds along the banks of the Yangtze River. Though the sinking *Panay* was clearly marked by American flags as belonging to the United States, the Japanese pilots

continued their assault. Two American sailors and an Italian journalist were killed in the attack, which was filmed by a news reporter.

Politicians and citizens in the United States reacted angrily to the news, and for a moment the two nations appeared on the verge of warfare. Franklin Roosevelt knew that he could do little to show American power in China and thus did not want to start a war, while the Japanese government feared that the United States would cut off shipment of valuable scrap iron and oil to Japan. With neither side eager to fight, a peaceful solution emerged. Roosevelt demanded that Japan offer a public apology and pay more than $2 million in damages. Tokyo agreed, and Roosevelt accepted the explanation that

The casket of a Panay victim is prepared for return to the United States. Japanese aircraft attacked the gunboat, though they claimed it was a mistake.

the Japanese pilots had incorrectly identified the *Panay* as a Chinese vessel. Though both sides avoided war at this time, the affair soured relations between Japan and the United States.

The U.S. Military Expands

The *Panay* incident handed Roosevelt reasons for strengthening his military. One month after the gunboat sank, Roosevelt asked for and received from Congress a 20 percent increase in funds for the navy so the nation could build enough ships to station a fleet in both the Atlantic and Pacific oceans. At the same time he requested that American weapons and aircraft manufacturers stop bargaining with Japan, and he reduced the amount of important products, such as scrap iron, oil, and cotton, sent to Japan from the United States.

In October 1939 Roosevelt changed the Pacific Fleet's home base from San Diego, California, to Pearl Harbor, Hawaii. With this move Roosevelt advanced his navy 2,500 miles (4,000km) closer to Japan and transformed the United States into a more powerful presence in the Pacific. Roosevelt hoped that this series of moves would send a message to the Japanese that the United States opposed Japan's actions in Asia and would react with even more strength in the future.

Meanwhile, when Hitler overran Western Europe in the spring of 1940 and threatened to knock Great Britain out of the war, Congress voted more money for the military. Shipbuilders increased their output, and aircraft plants worked to produce fifty thousand new aircraft. In September 1940, Congress passed the first peacetime draft in the nation's history in an attempt to expand the military.

Most military leaders dismissed the notion that the Japanese would launch an attack against the American fleet at Pearl Harbor. Though they developed a plan to cover the possibility, few believed it would occur. They expected an attack to take place at some point in East Asia, such as the Philippines, and ignored the notion that the Japanese were capable of striking Pearl Harbor while their forces were engaged elsewhere. Army chief of staff General George C. Marshall told Roosevelt in May 1941 that Pearl Harbor was "the strongest fortress in the world." He added:

> Enemy carriers, naval escorts and transports [trying to approach Pearl Harbor] will begin to come under air attack at a distance of approximately 750 miles. This attack will increase in intensity until within 200 miles of the objective, [and] the enemy forces will be subject to all types of bombardment closely supported by our most modern pursuit. An invader would face more than 35,000 troops backed by coast defense guns and antiaircraft artillery.[7]

This optimistic evaluation would shortly be tested and found wanting.

In the final week of November, Admiral Husband E. Kimmel, the commander in chief of the Pacific Fleet, asked his operations officer, Captain Charles

McMorris, what the chances were that the Japanese would hit Pearl Harbor. "None,"[8] McMorris confidently replied. Should the Japanese be so bold, few Americans believed they would pose much of a threat. "The United States Navy can defeat the Japanese Navy any place, any time,"[9] stated one United States senator.

American Defense Moves in the Pacific

Although small numbers of American troops filtered to various American possessions in the Pacific, the country did not have enough forces to stop Japan. As open conflict neared, only four hundred marines and navy personnel defended Wake Island; the same number guarded Guam. Most of the navy's 347 warships steamed in Atlantic waters. Should Japan attack, it was not likely that American troops could do anything but fight as long as possible, and then surrender.

Top American military planners held one ace in their hands—army and navy codebreakers had figured out Japan's code for sending messages from Tokyo to overseas embassies. From 1935 to 1939 they

Marines in the Pacific travel in a Water Buffalo vessel. The small forces the United States maintained in the Pacific prior to World War II would not last long in battle.

German and Japanese officials toast their alliance in the Tripartite Pact of 1940.

intercepted and read most of the messages. The Japanese switched codes in March 1939, but American codebreakers, aided by the theft of secret material from a Japanese embassy office in Washington, D.C., were able to crack the new code and learn of Japanese intentions before they acted.

Buried in the hundreds of decoded messages were signs pointing to Pearl Harbor as the focus of Japanese operations, but just as many indicated Singapore, the Philippines, or other locations. In the guessing game that unfolded, most analysts predicted what they considered the obvious—an attack in the western Pacific, never dreaming the Japanese could steal across the ocean to hit the American naval base in Hawaii.

Momentum for War Builds

Intercepted messages informed the United States of Japan's advance into French Indochina, south of China. Since Hitler had defeated France and the Netherlands, and appeared to be about to knock Great Britain out of the war, Japan saw an opportunity to seize European possessions in the Pacific and gain control of their valuable resources. Japan began by applying pressure on a weakened France to allow them to place troops in Indochina. While the Japanese claimed that the forces were necessary to protect their southern flank in China, Japan was actually interested in obtaining Indochina's vast natural resources and possessing a base from which to push southward against British-held Burma and Malaya. Japanese troops moved into Indochina in July 1941.

In September 1940 the Japanese signed the Tripartite Pact with Germany and Italy. The agreement bound each party to declare war on any nation that joined the war against one of the three. The three hoped this alliance would keep the United States from entering the conflict. In response to the Japanese expansion and the new pact, President Roosevelt cut off all trade with Japan, including the flow of oil. He promised to maintain this embargo until Japan withdrew from both China and Indochina and quit the Tripartite Pact.

In light of Roosevelt's orders to stop the flow of oil, Japanese leaders could follow one of two paths. They could reach a settlement with the United States and re-open the supply line from that nation, or they could continue their present policy of overseas expansion and risk war with the United States. Since they held only enough oil and supplies to last for eighteen to thirty-six months of war, the leaders had to decide on which course to adopt and how best to act on it.

Yamamoto's Plan

Admiral Isoroku Yamamoto, commander of the Japanese Combined Fleet, had the answer. As the fastest-rising star in the Japanese navy, Yamamoto urged the development of more aircraft carriers and naval air power. Because of his efforts, the Japanese navy boasted six large aircraft carriers by the time open warfare took place.

Though Admiral Isoroku Yamamoto was reluctant to go to war, he proposed the plan to strike the United States at Pearl Harbor.

Unlike most others at that time, Yamamoto feared the awesome strength of the United States. As a young officer he had traveled to the nation and marveled at the many factories and oil fields. He repeatedly reminded his more warlike comrades that as Japan could never defeat America, Japan should not attack America. Yamamoto so strongly warned against this that in 1939 his superiors ordered him to sea to protect him from being murdered.

Yamamoto saw the rising desire for war among his comrades and decided that if he could not prevent it, he could at least influence how the war would be fought. In early 1941 he wrote his friend, Rear Admiral Takejiro Onishi, chief of staff of the Eleventh Air Fleet, "If we are to have war with America, we will have no hope of winning unless the U.S. fleet in Hawaiian waters can be destroyed."[10]

Yamamoto proposed a stunning plan to strike the American navy at its base in Pearl Harbor. He argued that only by delivering a strong opening blow to the enemy could the Japanese gain the time to grab the Pacific and Asian lands they desired and succeed in driving the United States to the bargaining table. He warned that the outcome had to be decided on the first day or all would be lost.

Yamamoto's Fascination with the United States

Isoroku Yamamoto took advantage of two trips to the United States to learn about the country that would be his future adversary. During his first trip, which began in 1919, his main purpose was to learn all he could about the United States. He studied English and petroleum resources at Harvard University near Boston, Massachusetts. He also traveled to Chicago and Detroit, where the massive stockyards and automotive assembly lines awed the visitor. Little in Japan, he noted, matched the immense natural resources he saw in the great American Midwest.

Yamamoto spent much of his free time reading books about the United States, focusing on biographies of leaders and inventors. One person that impressed the young officer was Abraham Lincoln. Yamamoto recommended to associates that if they wanted to learn about the United States, they must read Carl Sandburg's biography of the Civil War president. Yamamoto liked that Lincoln, while being a great leader, also admitted that he made mistakes. Yamamoto wrote of the American president, "A man of real purpose always puts his faith in himself" even when he errs, but making mistakes "does not detract from his greatness because a man is not a god. Making errors is part of the attractiveness of a human being; it inspires a feeling of warmth and arouses admiration and devotion. In this way Lincoln was a very human person. Without this quality, one cannot lead others. Only if people have this quality can they forgive each other's mistakes and assist each other."

Six years later Yamamoto returned to the United States for his second visit, this time as the Japanese naval attaché in Washington, D.C., the officer assigned to study the U.S. Navy. During this stint he was especially interested in naval aviation and aircraft carriers. As a result of his two trips, Yamamoto had a deeper appreciation for the capabilities of the United States. He made certain never to underestimate his future enemy.

Edwin P. Hoyt. *Yamamoto*. New York: McGraw-Hill, 1990, p. 58.

Onishi took the plans to his friend Commander Minoru Genda, a brilliant young pilot. The two concluded that Yamamoto's suggestion made sense and began studying ways to attack Pearl Harbor. Genda turned to his trusted friend, the commander of all air groups aboard the carrier *Akagi*, Commander Mitsuo Fuchida, and mentioned his desire that Fuchida lead the air groups in a strike against Pearl Harbor. At a loss for words, Fuchida wondered whether Genda was teasing him, as no one had considered distant Pearl Harbor to be a likely target for attack. It stood too far away and was likely to be too heavily defended to be triumphantly assaulted.

To be successful, Fuchida knew that his navy had to create a weapon that would sink American carriers and battleships anchored in Pearl Harbor's shallow waters. When dropped from aircraft, current torpedoes would plunge too deeply and only strike the muddy bottom, thus lessening the weapon's impact. A committee studying the problem arrived at a solution; by attaching wooden stabilizers on the torpedo fins, they lessened the depth at which the weapon would operate.

They also studied the element of surprise that was necessary for the attacking force, which meant the carriers had to draw within 200 miles (320km) of Hawaii without being spotted. Fuchida and others solved this problem by selecting a northern route from Japan to Hawaii. Though passing through areas that featured more storms, the little-used path would take the ships away from more heavily traveled routes where other ships might spot them.

Many military leaders opposed such a daring plan. After all, they wondered, how could a huge array of ships sneak across the Pacific and unleash a surprise attack on a foe that was sure to be prepared? Yamamoto had scrutinized reports from agents operating in Hawaii and noticed that the American fleet was in port every weekend and in a state of reduced readiness. He believed that a Japanese fleet could inch toward Hawaii and hit the enemy when they least expected it. When the highly respected Yamamoto threatened to resign if his plan was not adopted, in November 1941 the navy general staff agreed to the changes.

Yamamoto realized that he was advising his nation to take a huge gamble. The United States possessed ten times the capacity to manufacture weapons than did Japan, which meant that they would certainly win any drawn-out struggle. Japan would have to deliver a knockout blow in the early stages or face defeat. Yamamoto claimed that in the first six to twelve months of fighting, the war would be in Japan's favor, but, he quickly added, "I have absolutely no confidence in what would happen if it went on for one or two years."[11]

The War Draws Closer

Army and navy leaders in Japan agreed that if diplomats could not convince President Roosevelt to lift the embargo on oil and other products by the first week in November, they would start their operations against the United States and the European powers. While talks continued, the military prepared for war.

Japanese spies in Hawaii radioed crucial information to Tokyo. Ensign Takeo Yoshikawa obtained most of his intelligence by walking out to Pearl Harbor and observing the ships that entered and departed. He gathered information by sitting in a restaurant located on a hill overlooking the harbor, and once snapped photographs of ships and installations while accompanying a group of tourists on an airplane trip over the harbor. He also noted how long the vessels remained at sea, where each ship docked, and for how long. He especially noted that most ships returned to Pearl Harbor on weekends so the crews could enjoy time ashore.

In the meantime, Japanese diplomats negotiated, telling their American counterparts that if Roosevelt restarted oil shipments to Japan, the nation would halt its military action in Indochina. Alerted by intercepted messages that

Commander Fuchida and the Japanese Militarist Spirit

The military commanded enormous respect from the population in Japan in the 1920s and 1930s. Schoolchildren collected coins in a drive to finance the construction of a battleship, and it was deemed an honor to serve the emperor. Thus, when Mitsuo Fuchida reached the age of seventeen, he gladly entered his two years of service. His enlistment was celebrated in a party hosted by the residents of his hometown.

Rigorous military training instilled discipline and an aversion to surrendering. Instructors taught Fuchida that loyalty to one's unit, faith in commanding officers, and an indomitable spirit would defeat any foe, no matter how well-armed it might be. Attacking, even in circumstances that produced ghastly casualties, was preferred to surrendering or pulling back. Fuchida trained fourteen hours a day, six days a week, under the watch of dictatorial officers who answered complaints with punishment. He and other men would embark on marches of twenty-five miles wearing gear that weighed two-thirds of their own body weights, then run the final mile to prove they still had reserves of strength.

Fuchida's life belonged to the emperor, and to suffer defeat or surrender was considered an insult to the emperor and shamed the soldier's family. His behavior was governed by the ancient samurai tradition known as *bushido*, which means "way of the warrior." The samurai were honored fighters in Japan's history, and soldiers of the imperial army were expected to follow their example. A soldier like Fuchida could attain no higher glory than to die in battle.

Secretary of State Cordell Hull, left, warned President Franklin Roosevelt that military action would be necessary to settle issues with Japan.

Japanese troops were already on transports bound for the Dutch East Indies and Southeast Asia, areas containing vital natural resources that the United States had long imported, the American government turned down the proposal. In late November Secretary of State Hull warned Roosevelt and his cabinet that diplomacy could not settle the issue and that military action would be required. War warnings raced from the nation's capital to military posts throughout the Pacific.

Concern increased in November when American intelligence discovered that the Japanese had again changed their codes. Suddenly unable to understand the enemy's messages, intelligence officers could only guess at the whereabouts of the Japanese aircraft carriers. A worried Kimmel asked his fleet intelligence officer, Captain Edwin T. Layton, "Do you mean to say they could be rounding Diamond Head [a large crater in Oahu that is a popular Hawaiian landmark and tourist attraction] and you wouldn't know it?"

"I would hope they could be sighted before that,"[12] replied Layton.

War Warnings

With their attempt to negotiate failing, the Japanese turned to their military as the only way to avoid being economically strangled. Though Roosevelt made one final attempt to keep talks going by sending a personal note to Japanese emperor Hirohito on December 6, in part because he needed more time to strengthen American military forces in the Pacific, no reply followed. American codebreakers then intercepted a message to Japanese diplomats in Washington ordering them to destroy sensitive documents and to present a note to the United States at 1:00 P.M. on December 7 severing diplomatic negotiations. Roosevelt said to his top adviser, Harry Hopkins, that it meant war.

A war warning was sent to every American military post in the Pacific. The message bluntly stated, "NEGOTIATIONS

Dangerous Flight

As he related in his book *The Flying Guns*, fighter pilot Lt. Clarence E. Dickinson and his rear seat man, W.C. Miller, flew toward Pearl Harbor from the aircraft carrier *Enterprise* early in the morning on December 7. They shared lighthearted banter as they approached Hawaii, and Miller remarked that of the twenty-one men that went through radio school together, he was the only one not to crash. "Hope you won't get me wet today, Sir," joked Miller.

As they neared Pearl Harbor their amiable chat halted when they noticed two columns of smoke. The pair was not at first alarmed, as farmers often set fire to sugarcane fields, but when they drew closer they noticed antiaircraft fire peppering the sky and Japanese aircraft darting all around. They had flown directly into the opening moments of the December 7 attack.

A group of four or five Japanese fighters focused on Dickinson's plane, puncturing the aircraft's fuselage and injuring Miller. "Mr. Dickinson," shouted Miller, "I have been hit once, but I think I have got one of [them]." The Japanese drew within 100 feet and stitched the wing with their machine gun bullets, igniting a fire in one of the engines and mortally wounding Miller.

With the plane spiraling out of control, Dickinson parachuted and landed on a dirt road west of the marine base at Ewa Field. He hitched a ride to Pearl Harbor from a pair of residents. As they arrived, scenes of destruction greeted them, with battleships resting on their sides and smoke billowing skyward from numerous vessels.

Dickinson's peaceful Sunday morning ended with the death of his friend and the loss of his aircraft. War had handed a rude welcome to the naval officer.

Clarence E. Dickinson. *The Flying Guns*. New York: Charles Scribner's Sons, 1943, pp. 1, 12.

WITH JAPAN LOOKING TOWARD STA-BILIZATION OF CONDITIONS IN THE PACIFIC HAVE CEASED. AN AGGRES-SIVE MOVE BY JAPAN IS EXPECTED WITHIN THE NEXT FEW DAYS."[13] Since the Japanese military had sent large forces to Indochina, 6,000 miles (9,600km) west of Hawaii, United States military commanders dismissed the idea that Pearl Harbor was endangered. Most predicted that war would start in the Philippines or Southeast Asia. As a precaution against sabotage, though, all aircraft at Hawaiian airfields were neatly arranged in rows so they could be more easily guarded.

"Everything was ready," wrote *Time* magazine in its final issue published before the war began. "From Rangoon to Honolulu, every man was at battle stations." The magazine added, "A vast array of armies, of navies, of air fleets were stretched now in the position of track runners, in the tension of the moment before the starter's gun. A bare chance of peace remained—of a kind of peace very close to war but not quite war."[14]

Chapter Three

The Attack Opens

In late November six Japanese aircraft carriers, protected by two battleships, three cruisers, and nine destroyers, moved toward a remote harbor in the Kurile Islands, the northernmost region of the Japanese home islands, to prepare for the secret voyage across the Pacific. Under strict radio silence and masked by thick fog, the fleet sailed on November 26. A patrol boat stationed at the bay's entrance flashed the message, "Good luck on your mission" as crews shouted "Banzai!"[15] Every man aboard the departing vessels, most believing they would not return from the daring venture, took one last look at their beloved homeland.

The Japanese Approach

The armada of warships, under the command of vice admiral Chuichi Nagumo, headed along a rarely traveled northern route across the Pacific to escape being seen by foreign steamers. The ships used high-grade fuel to produce less smoke and stored their own garbage rather than tossing it overboard so as to avoid leaving any trail behind. Three fleet submarines patrolled the waters in advance of Nagumo's ships, and twenty-seven other submarines arrived at positions ringing Oahu, the island locale of Pearl Harbor. Five carried two-man midget submarines that would, in the hours before the attack, detach from their mother submarines, sneak into Pearl Harbor, and launch their two torpedoes (a total of ten) at American warships.

On December 6 Admiral Nagumo refueled his ships for the final run into Oahu, then received a final report from the Japanese consulate in Hawaii on American warships then in Pearl Harbor. Though all the battleships and numerous other vessels remained in their berths, the American aircraft carriers were somewhere at sea rather than in port. "It is most regrettable that no carriers are in,"[16]

On December 7, 1941, Japanese bombers headed to Pearl Harbor on the Hawaiian island of Oahu, where U.S. military ships were docked.

said a disappointed Minoru Genda to Fuchida. Nagumo's aviators would have plenty of targets, but unfortunately they would not have the chance to sink the enemy's carriers.

Shortly before dawn on December 7 the fleet arrived at its launch point 230 miles (368km) due north of Oahu and readied its aircraft for attack. Flight crews went to briefing rooms to receive the final reports before heading to their planes, and Nagumo shook Fuchida's hand and declared his confidence in the pilot.

Pilots put on the "thousand-stitch" belts that had been made for good luck by family and friends back home, ate special breakfasts of rice boiled with red beans, and toasted to good fortune. They then packed rice balls, pickled plums,

and chocolate to munch on during the flight to Pearl Harbor.

Japanese flyers and sailors struggled to contain their excitement. One seaman named Kuamoto wrote, "An air attack on Hawaii! A dream come true. What will the people at home think when they hear the news? Won't they be excited! I can see them clapping their hands and shouting with joy! We would teach the Anglo-Saxon [American] scoundrels a lesson!"[17]

With every possible step completed, Fuchida walked to his aircraft, where the senior officer of his maintenance unit handed him a white *hachimaki*, a cloth headband signifying good fortune. "This is a present from the maintenance crews," he told Fuchida. "May I ask that you take it along to Pearl Harbor?"[18] An emotional Fuchida happily accepted the gift and attached it to his cap.

Yamamoto sent his attacking fleet one final message, the same one used in battle thirty-six years earlier by Admiral Heihachiro Togo when Japan annihilated the Russian fleet at Tsushima during the Russo-Japanese War: "ON THIS ONE BATTLE RESTS THE FATE OF OUR NATION. LET EVERY MAN DO HIS UTMOST."[19] Cheering men lined the flight deck as each aircraft lifted from the carriers, hoping to raise the chances of success with their support. Within fifteen minutes the 183 fighters, bombers, and torpedo planes assembled in the still-dark sky and turned toward their target.

In front of the forty-nine bombers he commanded, Fuchida scoured the sky about him to make certain the other planes flew in the proper locations. To his satisfaction, 440 yards (400m) to his right and a little below him flew the forty torpedo planes led by Lieutenant Commander Shigeharu Murata, while at a similar distance to his left and slightly above him flashed the fifty-one dive-bombers guided by Lieutenant Commander Kakuichi Takahashi. Flying cover for the

A Jubilant Reaction

Admiral Matome Ugaki, chief of staff of the Japanese Combined Fleet and one of Yamamoto's most trusted advisers, kept a detailed diary during the war in which he expressed his joys, concerns, hopes, and fears. The attack against Pearl Harbor produced this entry for December 7, 1941.

"The long-anticipated day has arrived at last. I knew that the attack order had been issued to the two hundred planes of our task force which had been approaching Hawaii, and the first attack on Pearl Harbor was under way."

Ugaki spent part of the day listening to radio transmissions broadcast from Hawaii by both Japanese and American combatants. He wrote that he "listened with attention to every telegram: 'I torpedoed enemy battleship with great war result,' or 'I bombed Hickam Airfield and got a great war result,' which were wired by our friendly planes, as well as enemy wireless messages which were most interesting. Enemy consternation [worry] is beyond description. It is their breakfast time. While they were at their breakfast table, great masses of Japanese airplanes came like bolts from the blue; I can imagine their utter surprise."

Matome Ugaki. *Fading Victory: The Diary of Admiral Matome Ugaki, 1941–1945*. Pittsburgh: University of Pittsburgh Press, 1991, p. 43.

entire force and tasked with the job of keeping American planes away was Lieutenant Commander Shigeru Itaya and his forty-three fighters. Fuchida noticed that as the sun was peeking over the eastern horizon and wings all about him glittered in the December 7 sunrise.

United States Ignores Warning Signs

In the hours before the bombing, military personnel and civilians in Hawaii went about their business with little clue that their lives were about to change. The evening before, army lieutenant general Walter C. Short, who, as commander of the Hawaiian Department was the top army general on the island, was returning from dinner with his wife and friends. As they drove on a road along Pearl Harbor, the U.S. fleet spread out below in all its glory, with sleek battleships and cruisers occupying the best positions, like kings perched upon their thrones. Short gazed at the scene and said, "Isn't that a beautiful sight?" After pausing for a moment, he added, "And what a target they would make."[20]

In the early hours of the morning on December 7, developments occurred with lightning speed. At 3:42 A.M. Ensign R.C. McCloy aboard the minesweeper

Five Japanese midget submarines, like the one pictured here, snuck into Pearl Harbor.

Controversy

Some historians claim that, rather than having been surprised by the Japanese attack at Pearl Harbor, President Roosevelt actually knew from intercepted messages sent out by the Japanese carriers that the assault was coming three days before it occurred. In these historians' opinions Roosevelt, who knew that the nation would join the World War II fighting sooner or later, decided not to act on the information because he wanted the Japanese to fire the first shots.

However, other historians dismiss these claims as the unfounded utterances of a handful of Roosevelt detractors. They state that the Japanese carriers never sent any messages in the days before the assault and wonder why an American president would so willingly sacrifice American lives. If Roosevelt did have prior knowledge of the attack, he certainly would have relayed the information to Admiral Kimmel so that he could successfully repel the enemy fleet. A victory in a surprise attack would certainly have been better for Roosevelt and the nation than the disastrous defeat that unfolded.

USS *Condor*, spotted a periscope two miles out while on a routine sweep of the harbor entrance. He sent word to the USS *Ward*, a destroyer on night patrol, which embarked on a two-hour search but saw nothing. Neither the *Condor* nor the *Ward* thought to alert headquarters about the supposed sighting.

At 4:47 the antitorpedo netting that blocked the entrance into the harbor was opened to allow the passage of a mine-sweeper and two other vessels. The five Japanese midget submarines took advantage of the opening to sneak into the harbor and steam toward their attack positions.

They did not remain concealed for long. At 6:33 a navy patrol plane spotted something trailing the USS *Antares*, a repair ship inside the harbor. The pilot dropped smoke flares to mark the location, then alerted authorities. Twelve minutes later the *Ward* dropped depth charges, or underwater bombs, on one of the midget submarines, sinking the tiny vessel. This time the *Ward*'s skipper, Lieutenant William Outerbridge, alerted headquarters, but Admiral Kimmel did not receive the news until after Japanese aircraft had already begun their attack.

In Washington, D.C., army general George Marshall noticed that the intercepted Japanese message stipulated that the note be handed to President Roosevelt precisely at 1:00 P.M. Marshall wondered whether that held any significance for the Pacific, where the sun would just be rising over Pearl Harbor, and he ordered an alert sent to Hawaii. Difficulties along the way slowed the message's arrival, which did not land on Kimmel's desk until after the attack had started.

Authorities received one final alert. At 7:02 A.M. the army radar station at Opana near Oahu's northern tip registered a large formation of aircraft approaching 137 miles (219km) to the north. Radar operators phoned in the information to Pearl Harbor, but were told it was nothing to be alarmed about. A unit of American B-17 bombers from the mainland

was expected that morning. It was undoubtedly those planes that the radar operators had spotted, they were told.

The Japanese Strike

Fuchida checked one final item as his planes winged toward Pearl Harbor. In hopes of learning the weather conditions over Hawaii and whether the skies over the ships were clear or cloudy, he switched the radio direction finder to tune into a Hawaiian radio station. He at first heard nothing but music, but then grinned when an announcer stated that while clouds

Battleship Row at Pearl Harbor served as a berth for major battleships. They were clustered together, which made them easy targets for Japanese bombing.

had formed over Oahu's mountains, conditions were clear over Pearl Harbor.

"What a windfall for us!" he later wrote. "No matter how careful the planning, a more favorable situation could not have been imagined."[21] Fuchida had done all he could to ensure a victory. The rest would depend upon surprise and the American response.

After approaching the northern tip of Oahu at 7:40 A.M., Fuchida's aircraft split for their runs into the harbor. His dive-bombers ascended to 13,000 feet (3,900m), the torpedo aircraft dropped close to sea level, and the level bombers dipped barely below the clouds. The attackers sped by Oahu's northern tip, veered right, and flew down the island's west coast, entering their final approach to the harbor. Fuchida could not have been more delighted with the sight that unfolded.

"Presently the harbor itself became visible across the central Oahu plain, a film of morning mist hovering over it. I peered intently through my binoculars at the ships riding peacefully at anchor. One by one I counted them. Yes, the battleships were there all right, eight of them!"[22] A quick scan showed no trace of the aircraft carriers, but the ninety-four vessels that floated peacefully in the harbor, including the eight battleships and nine cruisers, provided Fuchida with more than enough targets. Making his task easier, many of the ships he viewed below were berthed in clusters of two to five ships, a startling lapse in judgment in his opinion. Normally ships would anchor hundreds of yards apart to make an attack more complicated and to lessen the chances of one bomb damaging more than one vessel.

In the middle of the harbor lay Ford Island, a spot of land that housed an airfield and provided berths for major warships along its eastern and western shorelines. Seven of the eight battleships floated along the eastern shore at Battleship Row, while a mixture of cruisers, old battleships used in training, and a seaplane tender (a floating mechanic shop to repair parts) rested along the western shore. In the waters to the north and west floated seven groups of destroyers, so tightly anchored together that Fuchida's bombs and torpedoes could hardly miss hitting something. To the south rested ships in repair docks, including the battleship *Pennsylvania*, immense oil depots containing the vital fuel that would propel the fleet, and the naval hospital. Four airfields cradled Pearl Harbor in what was expected to be a sturdy aerial defense line—Wheeler Field lay to the north, Kanehoe guarded the eastern approaches, Hickam Field the south, and Ewa Field the west. Four hundred aircraft sat on those airfields, parked wingtip to wingtip in an effort to better safeguard them from sabotage.

More stunning to the Japanese was the lack of American aircraft or antiaircraft fire to meet them. Fuchida had expected to fight his way in, but nothing had yet risen in opposition. "Pearl Harbor was still asleep in the morning mist," wrote Lieutenant Commander Itaya, in charge of the fighters that escorted the other aircraft. "It was calm and serene inside the harbor, not even a trace of smoke from the ships at Oahu. The orderly groups of barracks [sleeping quarters], the wriggling white line of the automobile road climbing up to the mountain-top; fine objectives of attack in all directions. In line with these, inside the harbor, were important ships of the Pacific Fleet, strung out and anchored two ships side by side in an orderly manner."[23]

Fuchida sent the prearranged signal, "*Tora, tora, tora*" to indicate he had achieved complete surprise, and then at 7:49 ordered his planes to attack. The dive-bombers divided into two groups to attack three airfields protecting Pearl Harbor while the torpedo planes and level bombers flew toward the ships. Within ten minutes after the first bombs struck Hickam and Wheeler Fields, torpedoes and bombs turned Battleship Row into a fiery hellhole.

The First Bombs Hit

Unaware of the destruction that would shortly descend from the skies, American sailors at Pearl Harbor relaxed in the early Sunday morning hours. Since most had enjoyed liberty (being off-duty) the night before, many slept in. Others were getting ready to attend church services or enjoying a morning walk on the grounds. Stacked in neat rows along both sides of Ford Island, directly in the middle of Pearl Harbor, gleamed America's pride— the Pacific Fleet—including the mighty battleships on Battleship Row on the island's eastern shore. Their fellow navy, army, and marine personnel stationed across the Pacific might worry about the outbreak of war, but the men at Pearl Harbor had little reason for concern. A more secure spot could not be selected in the whole Pacific. War might erupt elsewhere, but no bombs would fall here.

Few ships were prepared to repel an attack on Pearl Harbor that day, for few expected one. Most of the captains and top officers of the ships were ashore, where the previous night they had enjoyed the luxuries of peacetime Oahu. Church bells rang throughout the island, summoning believers to 8:00 A.M. services, and crews aboard the ninety-four vessels prepared for another easygoing Sunday at Pearl Harbor.

Their peaceful world suddenly exploded at 7:55. Private first class William McCarthy knelt in a Catholic chapel when the sound of bombs broke the calm silence. As the church windows rattled from explosions, a soldier raced to the priest and whispered in his ears. "God bless you all," the priest said to the servicemen in the congregation, "the Japanese are attacking Pearl Harbor. Return to your units at once."[24]

Upon hearing the sound of explosions in the harbor below, Admiral Kimmel raced from his home at Makalapa Hill to view Japanese aircraft sweeping down on the ships and aircraft that composed his command. Frustration at being caught away from his command post while his men and ships were being attacked mixed with anger and surprise.

Navy captain John E. Lacouture, the assistant engineer on the USS *Blue*, a destroyer anchored north of Ford Island, had been invited to a party with top admirals at the Royal Hawaiian, the

A Japanese bomber flies over Pearl Harbor just prior to the attack. The Japanese struck in the early morning.

island's grandest hotel the night before. After an evening of laughing and dancing, Lacouture spent the night at a friend's house rather than return to his ship. Around 8:00 the next morning a friend rushed into his bedroom and started shaking the officer. "Wake up, wake up! The Japanese are attacking Pearl Harbor!"

"Are you crazy?" Lacouture said to his friend. "Go away, I'm sleepy."

It took the friend a few more moments, but helped by explosions that soon tore the air, a doubting Lacouture jumped out of bed, ran to his car, and sped toward Pearl Harbor. As he neared the water, one thought struck the assistant engineer as he witnessed scenes of destruction. "All I could think of was all my [naval academy] classmates and everything, and what had happened to them."[25]

Not far away the car that carried Captain D.C. Emerson of the battleship *Arizona* approached such high speeds that Emerson asked the driver to slow down. "Let's wait'll we get to Pearl to be killed,"[26] he joked.

Three minutes after the first bombs fell, Rear Admiral Patrick N. Bellinger broadcast a message from Kimmel's headquarters that soon raced around the world. "Air raid, Pearl Harbor—This is no drill."[27]

The United States had been swept into a war it knew had been coming, but in the most unexpected of places.

The weakest of responses from shore did little damage to the Japanese. One man blasted shots from his double-barreled shotgun as dive-bombers approached, while another fired his pistol as he rode away on a bicycle.

No matter how horrifying the scenes might be on shore, they paled when compared with the devastation unfolding in the harbor and at Oahu's airfields.

Shock in the Harbor

Disbelief briefly froze sailors and soldiers, civilians and generals throughout Oahu. In his sleeping quarters aboard the battleship *Arizona* Ensign G.S. Flannigan assumed the sound of an air raid siren was a joke until explosions rocked his ship. Pharmacist's mate second class Lee Soucy on the *Utah* had just completed breakfast when someone asked what a group of planes was doing flying on a Sunday morning. They all thought the marines must have scheduled an unusual training exercise. Nineteen-year-old marine private first class Art Wells on the *Pennsylvania* laughed in agreement when a sailor criticized the army's stupidity in

The USS Nevada *burns following the shocking attack by the Japanese. Band members on the* Nevada *were playing the "Star-Spangled Banner" when the bombing began, and they played to the finish before running for cover.*

holding gunnery practice on a Sunday morning. Their fun quickly melted away when the men realized they faced enemy bombs instead. "As I dodged others racing to their stations," Wells later said, "the expressions on faces registered shocked disbelief, anger and determination, and some had fear stamped indelibly [permanently] into their paled and drawn features. The mouths of others spewed curses as they damned the Japs in almost a scream."[28]

Band members playing "The Star-Spangled Banner" on the battleship *Nevada* assumed the planes that suddenly materialized were part of a training exercise and continued playing when aircraft started diving on nearby ships. They realized the gravity of the situation when a plane skimmed low across the harbor waters, dropped a torpedo at the *Arizona*, and continued directly over the musicians. Trained never to halt in the middle of the national anthem, the band members performed until the final note, then ran for cover.

The USS *Oklahoma*'s cook, nineteen-year-old Stephen Bower Young, could hardly wait to leave the battleship after breakfast. He and his girlfriend had planned a picnic to Nanakuli, a beautiful beach offering sand, surf, and gentle breezes. A bugle sounding over the ship's public address system suddenly changed Young's plans, not just for that day but for the next four years.

"What's going on?" everyone asked. When a voice boomed out, "All hands, man your battle stations!" Young and the other disbelieving sailors swore in reaction to what must be a drill, but stopped cussing when they realized this was war. "The harsh, excited voice on the PA system froze us in our tracks. 'All hands, man your battle stations! On the double! This is no drill! Get going—they're real bombs!'"[29]

Similar reactions momentarily froze men at the airfields ringing Pearl Harbor. At Ewa Field to the west, Captain Leonard Ashwell, the officer of the day, sounded the alarm when he noticed aircraft approaching the base. Twenty-one Japanese fighters swooped down and shot at the marine aircraft parked neatly in rows, setting off a string of explosions as first one and then another fighter burst into flames. One Japanese pilot fired at the car of base commander Lieutenant Colonel Claude Larkin as he hurried toward camp. Larkin leapt from the car into a ditch, allowed the Japanese to pass by, then returned to his vehicle to finish his journey. By the time he arrived, thirty-three of his forty-nine aircraft lay useless along the airfield, smoldering ruins spouting fire and smoke instead of bullets.

Two aircraft mechanics at Hickam Field south of Pearl Harbor believed that the planes they spotted were the expected American bombers arriving from the mainland. Mechanic Ted Conway said to Jesse Gaines, "We're going to have an air show." Gaines saw something drop from one of the aircraft and remarked that a wheel had fallen off one of the bombers. "Wheel, hell," blurted Conway, "they're Japs!"[30]

Twenty-three-year-old army technical sergeant Joseph A. Pesek waited outside Hickam Field for the 8:05 bus to take him to Honolulu for a golf outing at the Wai Lai Golf Course. While sitting on the bench, he noticed a large flight of aircraft approaching from the northwest. Believing the planes to be friendly, he let his thoughts drift to the day's round of golf but stopped his daydreaming when the aircraft began to turn into steep dives toward the harbor. Pesek watched a large torpedo-shaped bomb descend from the first plane and slowly drop toward a ship.

"As one after the other dropped their torpedoes, terrific explosions and flames were plainly visible. At the time, I thought it strange but possible that the Navy was conducting some sort of exercise and possibly destroying something over in the west locks where the target ship *Utah* and other old ships were moored." Pesek's hopes that all was routine ended when he obtained a closer view of the aircraft. "As the first plane pulled up only several hundred feet to my left with machine guns blazing, I saw the Rising Sun insignia on the wings and knew we were under attack."[31]

Oahu's First Experiences of the War

Similar responses occurred throughout Oahu, where civilians and nonmilitary personnel received rude awakenings after at first wondering what the fuss was about. Navy officer Hubert Dale Gano and his wife, Johnie, lay in bed at 8:00 A.M. chatting about what they might do on that gorgeous Hawaiian Sunday when loud explosions interrupted their discussion. They at first thought a navy plane had crashed in the neighborhood, but when

they rushed outside they found their neighbor, a navy doctor, peering at aircraft through binoculars. Dale Gano gazed more closely at the aircraft, which featured the rising sun emblem on their sides, and knew his nation was now at war.

When people attending a Catholic mass at the base chapel learned that the Japanese had struck, instead of singing a religious hymn they broke into "The Star-Spangled Banner." Private first class Joseph Nelles, a Catholic chaplain's assistant, was returning from mass when the Japanese bombs struck. He rushed back to get the Blessed Sacrament and was killed when a bomb destroyed the chapel.

Correspondent Joseph Harsch of the *Christian Science Monitor* had experienced air raids the year before when reporting on the war in Europe. His wife had asked him to describe the experience of being bombed by the enemy, but Harsch always had trouble finding the proper words to convey the desperation and helplessness that go with such attacks. Upon now hearing explosions from what he at first believed was a military exercise, he woke his wife and said, "Darling, you often have asked me what an air raid sounds like. Listen to this—it's a good imitation."[32]

Roy Vitousek, Jimmy Duncan, and Cornelia Fort found themselves trapped in a situation they could never have imagined. The three civilian pilots had been flying over Oahu enjoying a beautiful morning when the Japanese aircraft suddenly appeared. Caught unarmed in the midst of Fuchida's planes, they quickly turned their aircraft into steep dives and descended toward the water's surface as Japanese bullets filled the air around them. Fortunately, after firing the initial blast of bullets and convinced the three were of no concern, Fuchida's fighter pilots returned to shepherding the bombers and torpedo planes toward Pearl Harbor. The three landed safely, rattled from their experience at being among the earliest targets of Japan's assault.

Observing the opening moments of the attack from his aerial post, Fuchida tried to control his excitement, but the sight of bombs exploding underwater alongside the battleships overwhelmed the veteran officer. Here he was, over Oahu, with a dream scene unfolding before his eyes. In his attack, he had gotten the element of surprise that all had hoped for but few expected, and now bombs and bullets tore apart American aircraft and battleships.

While the destruction brought joy to Fuchida and his pilots, they aroused very different emotions for their targets—the sailors, marines, and army members suffering on the exploding ships and bomb-riddled airfields.

Chapter Four

The Agony of Battleship Row

From their place in the sky, Commander Fuchida and his pilots dropped bombs on battleships and airfields, cruisers and docks. Theirs was an impersonal fight, one that pitted their talents at directing bombs and bullets at seagoing vessels or dirt airstrips. Aboard each ship and stationed at every airfield, however, were young men like Corporal B.C. Nightingale, Cook Third Class Doris "Dorie" Miller, and Captain Mervyn S. Bennion, whose later memories reflect some of the confusion and horror of the day. For them and the thousands of other Americans at Pearl Harbor that day, there was nothing impersonal about those deadly missiles dropped by the Japanese to kill them. This was reality in its most frightening form.

The Destruction Begins

Fuchida was surprised by the lack of opposition his planes at first faced in attacking such an important military base. He assumed he would have to fight his way in, but the attack had been virtually unopposed. The Japanese had handily flown deep into the heart of the American defense, which, Fuchida noted, "had been turned into complete chaos [disorder] in a very short time."[33]

No one would argue with the Japanese commander's conclusion. Within minutes of the start of the attack, Murata's torpedo planes descended close to the water's surface, roared toward Battleship Row, and released one torpedo that struck the *Nevada*, three that hit the USS *California*, nine that slammed into the USS *West Virginia*, and twelve that tore into the *Oklahoma*. Before most sailors had a chance to reach their battle stations, the ships they served had been transformed into blazing infernos of mangled metal.

In orderly fashion the Japanese aircraft completely destroyed Battleship Row, where seven of the eight active battleships

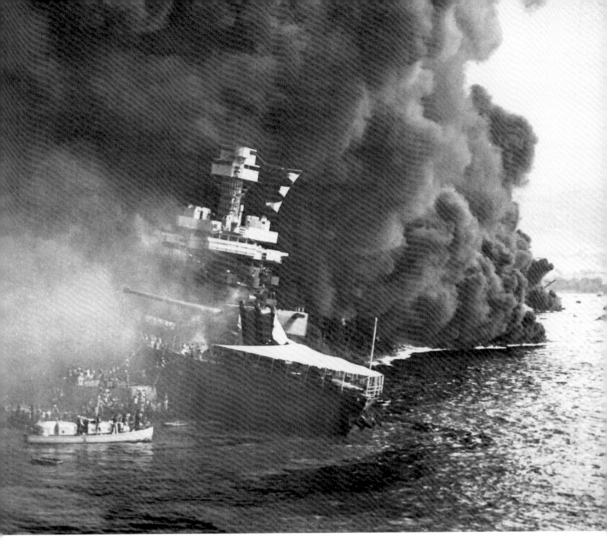

The USS California *was hit by three torpedoes as it sat in Battleship Row. The crew had to abandon ship.*

of the fleet floated in a straight line stretching northeast to southwest along Ford Island's eastern shore. At the top and bottom of the line, standing about 880 yards (800m) apart, rested the *Nevada* and *California*. In between those two, five other battleships and one repair ship anchored in three pairs of two. Tightly packed together in Pearl Harbor's restricted waters, the five battleships in the middle received the worst damage.

At the northern end one torpedo and two aerial bombs smashed into the *Nevada*, but the ship was able to raise steam and get under way during the attack. At the southern end of the line, the *California* listed to port (a ship's left side) from torpedo hits and from a bomb that ignited a fire that immediately killed fifty crew members. The ship slowly settled to the harbor's bottom, with much of her main deck still above water.

An Early Capture

Japan posted spies in Hawaii to learn whatever they could about American naval operations at the vital base. On December 7 secret agent Takeo Yoshikawa ate his breakfast in Honolulu when suddenly the windows of his residence started to rattle. When he rushed outside, he saw aircraft bearing Japanese markings. Yoshikawa then raced to the home of a Japanese consul.

"Mr. Kita," he shouted. "They've done it!"

Tears filled their eyes as they spotted the image of black smoke billowing skyward from Pearl Harbor. Yoshikawa, knowing that American law enforcement agents would soon arrive to detain him and the other workers in the Japanese consulate, locked himself in the building's code room and began burning Japanese code books in a washtub.

Ten minutes after he started, an American shouted, "Open the door!" Federal Bureau of Investigation (FBI) agents had come to take Yoshikawa into custody. "Good-bye to the days of my youth—forever," thought Yoshikawa.

John Toland. *The Rising Sun*. New York: Random House, 1970, pp. 277–278.

Devastation on the *Arizona*

The battleships that were anchored in pairs attracted the most attention. While the *Nevada* was able to move away from her berth, only 75 feet (22.5m) to her south the *Arizona* had no chance to start her engines. Tied to the inboard side (closest to land) along the USS *Vestal*, a repair ship, the *Arizona* was only partially shielded from the enemy torpedoes by the smaller *Vestal*. Before the crew could reach their battle stations, the ship took several torpedo and bomb hits, the most damaging of which was a bomb that ripped a hole in the deck and exploded in one of the ship's ammunition storerooms. An immense fireball shot 500 feet (150m) into the air. The blast from the bomb knocked down men standing on nearby battleships and shook Fuchida's aircraft as he circled above.

"We were about to begin our second bombing run when there was a colossal [huge] explosion in battleship row," recalled the Japanese commander. "A huge column of dark red smoke rose to 3,300 feet. The shock wave was felt even in my plane several miles away from the harbor."[34]

Onlookers thought they saw the ship actually jump out of the water from the violent explosions. Hundreds of men died instantly, with many more killed in the next few moments, including a rear

The USS Arizona, *devastated by the Japanese attack, sinks in the harbor.*

admiral and the captain of the ship. A second bomb plunged directly down one of the ship's smokestacks and exploded deep within the ship's insides, followed one after another by six other bombs that ripped into different sections of the doomed vessel.

"I was about three quarters of the way to the first platform on the mast when it seemed as though a bomb struck our quarterdeck," said marine corporal B.C. Nightingale. "I could hear shrapnel or fragments whistling past me. As soon as I reached the first platform, I saw Second

Lieutenant Simonsen lying on his back with blood on his shirt front. I bent over him and, taking him by the shoulders, asked if there was anything I could do. He was dead, or so nearly so that speech was impossible. Seeing there was nothing I could do for the Lieutenant, I continued to my battle station."[35]

"My battle station was on a forward 5-inch gun," said machinist's mate first class George D. Phraner, "and it was standard practice to keep only a limited amount of ammunition at the guns. There we were, the Japanese dropping bombs over us and we had no ammo. All the training and practicing for a year and when the real thing came we had no ammunition where we needed it. The gun captain pointed at me and said, 'You go aft (to the rear) and start bringing up the ammunition out of the magazines [storerooms].' The aft magazines were five decks below."

Phraner did not then realize it, but that order saved his life. As he worked in a section of the ship he had rarely entered, lifting ammunition powder and shells weighing about 90 pounds (41kg) each, a deafening roar shook the *Arizona*. One and half million pounds (68,1818kg) of gunpowder had exploded in a massive fireball that shattered the entire forward portion of the ship. "Only moments before I stood with my gun crew just a few feet from the center of the explosion. Admiral Kidd, Captain Van Valkenburgh, my whole gun crew was killed. Everyone on top,"[36] Phraner later recalled.

Arizona sailor Norman Lancaster returned fire as Japanese aircraft swarmed about his ship. "At first the planes would come in and dispose of their bombs and their torpedoes, and then they'd circle and come back and strafe [shoot at] us,"[37] he recalled. Shipmate Stuart Hedley dove under a gun to avoid the shrapnel and bullets and found a lieutenant already there, firing back with his .45 automatic pistol.

The battleship quickly settled to the bottom, half submerged in the oily waters, trapping most of the men who had survived the bombs and torpedoes. More than eleven hundred of the fifteen-hundred-man crew perished aboard the *Arizona*. The mostly sunken vessel remains there today as a memorial to the men who fought and died on December 7.

The *Tennessee* and *West Virginia*

Seventy-five feet (22.5m) to the south of the *Arizona* was the battleship *West Virginia*. Tied up inboard from the *West Virginia* and thus shielded by the battleship, the USS *Tennessee* avoided severe damage. Two bombs struck the vessel, but the ship suffered more from the debris and burning oil spewed from the giant explosions that tore apart the *Arizona*. Except for the *Arizona*, the inboard-anchored ships suffered less than the outboard ones, which were hit by most of the torpedoes dropped into the harbor.

The *West Virginia* was not as fortunate. In the opening moments of the attack, six torpedoes smacked into her port side, causing the ship to list, or tip, heavily and knocking out power throughout the ship. Captain Mervyn S. Bennion ordered

The USS West Virginia *and* USS Tennessee *were struck by several bombs. Great plumes of black smoke rose as the ships burned.*

Lieutenant C.V. Ricketts below to organize the efforts to prevent flooding. Ricketts made his way with difficulty through smoke-filled passageways, then directed a group of sailors as they turned valves that allowed water into the starboard (right) side to counterbalance the water gushing in through the torpedo holes on the port, or left side. When other sailors stretched cables to the adjoining *Tennessee*, the listing halted and the battleship slowly settled on the bottom rather than flipping over and trapping hundreds of crew members.

As the crew tried to save their ship, one of the bombs that struck the *Tennessee* rained ragged pieces of metal up to 5 inches (12.7cm) in diameter onto the *West Virginia*, fatally wounding Captain Bennion and many others. Moments later the *Arizona*'s ammunition magazines exploded, sending sheets of burning oil floating toward the *West Virginia*. "We had no water on board as the fire mains and machinery were out of commission and we were unable to do any fire fighting at all," said Lieutenant Commander T.T. Beattie, the ship's navigator. "I got

Word Home

Like many other men fighting in Hawaii, navy officer Paul Backus was concerned that his family back in Oklahoma would worry about his welfare. As related in Paul Stilwell's book, *Air Raid: Pearl Harbor*, Backus wanted to send a message home that he had survived, but all the normal channels of radio communications in Hawaii had been taken over for military needs and were unavailable. Frantic that his parents might be suffering over his safety, Backus contacted a girl he had been dating in Hawaii and asked her to try to get a cable bulletin home. On December 9 the navy handed out postcards for servicemen to send home, which Backus readily filled out and mailed. Happily, his girlfriend's cable arrived at the Backus home four days after the attack, ending a trying time for the Backus family.

into a motor launch to go to the stern of the ship to investigate the fire. The smoke was so heavy I could not see aft [back] of the bridge. As I got into the boat a sheet of flame swept on top of us and we barely managed to get free of the fire. I realized then that the ship was lost."[38]

The crew of the battleship *West Virginia* tried to mount a response to the swarms of enemy aircraft. A torpedo explosion hurled seaman second class Lewis E. LaGesse against the bulkhead and knocked him unconscious. His crewmates nearby thought he was dead and moved him to the starboard side and stacked him up with the dead bodies.

Cook third class Dorie Miller ran to the deck from below when the torpedoes struck. The African American kitchen worker from Texas carried the wounded Captain Bennion and other injured crew members to safer locations, then grabbed

a machine gun he had never before operated and began firing at the approaching aircraft. Miller, who later received the Navy Cross, the navy's second-highest award for bravery after the Medal of Honor, continued shooting until he ran out of ammunition, at which time he joined the others in abandoning the ship.

The *Maryland* and *Oklahoma*

Seventy-five feet (22.5m) away the next pair of ships—the USS *Maryland* and the *Oklahoma*—battled for their survival. Commander Fuchida had failed to locate his target, the battleship *Nevada*, in the increasing smoke and confusion that existed in the harbor—smoke from the gigantic *Arizona* explosion concealed the vessel. He scanned Battleship Row, selected the *Maryland*, and ordered his group to focus on that battleship instead.

Military officials stand atop the capsized USS Oklahoma *after it was hit in a Japanese attack, trapping 415 men in its holds below deck.*

After his plane dropped its four bombs, which Fuchida called "devils of doom," Fuchida lay on the floor of his aircraft to watch through a peephole. From the sky the *Maryland* seemed so distant and small that he wondered if the bombs would hit their target. As the bombs neared the water, he held his breath waiting for an explosion. "I forgot everything in the thrill of watching them fall toward the target. They became small as poppy seeds and finally disappeared just as tiny white flashes of smoke appeared on and near the ship." Bombs that barely miss a ship are easier to spot from the air as they create wave rings in the water, so when Fuchida only saw two such waves, he figured that the other two bombs had hit the *Maryland*. "I shouted, 'Two hits!' and rose from the floor of the plane."[39]

Fortunately the *Maryland*, shielded from torpedoes by its companion ship *Oklahoma*, suffered minor damage from the hits, especially when compared with its sister ships. From a crew of 1,604, only 4 were killed and 14 wounded.

The men aboard the *Oklahoma* were not as lucky. Three torpedoes struck in such rapid fashion that the ship immediately began flipping onto its side. Sailors had no time to prevent flooding and had to abandon ship to avoid being trapped below deck, but as they emerged and entered the water, Lieutenant Commander Itaya's fighters fired on the exposed Americans. Within eight minutes of the opening shot, the *Oklahoma* had slowly rolled onto her port side and settled to the harbor's bottom.

Aboard the *Oklahoma*, seaman James Bounds battled his emotions at the sight of his ship being hit and others rapidly sinking. He recalled, "The only thing they taught me going through training was that you could not sink a battleship."[40] But those three torpedoes quickly proved that idea wrong and fatally wounded the giant vessel.

Commander Jesse L. Kenworthy Jr. rushed about the wounded ship, gathering men in an attempt to mount a response to the Japanese. He recalled:

As I reached the upper deck, I felt a very heavy shock and heard a loud explosion and the ship immediately began to list to port. Oil and water descended on the deck and by the time I had reached the boat deck, the shock of two more explosions on the port side was felt. As I attempted to get to the Conning Tower over decks slippery with oil and water, I felt the shock of another very heavy explosion on the port side. By this time the ship was listing from 25 to 35 degrees and was continuing to list further. It was now obvious [clear] that the ship was going to continue to roll over and I climbed over the boat deck toward the starboard side. Men were beginning to come up from below through hatches and gun ports and from them it was learned that the ship was filling with water in many spaces below.[41]

Kenworthy's efforts, however gallant, could not stop the rivers of water from gushing into the ship's interior. Sailors, some hopelessly wounded and dying, engaged in a deadly race of exiting the ship's interior and reaching fresh air before the onrushing waters overwhelmed them. Many stuffed clothes and blankets into the ship's air vents to block the water's flow, but as soon as they plugged one leaking spot, another opened. As the waters rose, men trapped in different locations began to beat on the bulkheads (metal walls) in hopes of drawing help.

Catholic chaplain Lieutenant Aloysius Schmitt moved toward a door to evade the oncoming waters, but stopped to help three other men safely exit the room. By the time he had helped rescue the third sailor, the waters had trapped Schmitt inside, drowning the heroic priest.

The ship quickly rolled over and trapped 415 of the 1,354 men below deck. The lucky survivors slowly walked along the deck as the ship turned onto its side, then jumped into the harbor waters and swam to safety.

Sailors aboard other vessels or on land stared at the *Oklahoma* as it settled to the harbor bottom. The image of the once-mighty battleship now lying helplessly on the bottom was a sight no person soon forgot. "I felt like somebody kicked me in the stomach," said Ivan Harris. "You don't kill a battleship. They're impregnable, tough. But there was one over on its side."[42]

Damage Elsewhere

The eighth battleship, *Pennsylvania*, escaped serious harm because the vessel was in drydock in a different part of the harbor for repairs. Three dive-bombers and a handful of fighters attacked the ship, but crew managed to drive them away with antiaircraft guns.

In the vast confusion, the crew of one seaplane tender, the *Tangier*, reacted with amazing speed and efficiency. Commander Clifton A.F. Sprague had been fanatic about preparing his men for combat, and when war arrived, his crew responded bravely. The *Tangier*'s crew was at battle stations in moments, and the gunners returned fire on the Japanese before any other ship did that morning. "Everyone knew his job and went where he was supposed to,"[43] said seaman first class Leonard Barnes, the ship's radio operator.

While Sprague's gun crews filled the sky with antiaircraft fire, recording the first hits registered on Japanese aircraft, three Japanese torpedo planes approached from the north and released their torpe-

Captain Clifton A.F. Sprague commanded the USS Tangier. *When the attack began, his men responded with anti-aircraft fire on the Japanese planes. Sprague stayed on deck with his crew throughout the attack.*

A Rough Afternoon

Many survivors of the Pearl Harbor assault recorded their experiences that day for posterity. Ted LeBaron, a twenty-year-old navy bombsight repair and maintenance technician, was on Ford Island when the attack began. From his front-row seat on the island, which rests in the middle of Pearl Harbor, LeBaron observed amazing incidents that day and in the time following. He shared his memories on the website Pearl Harbor Remembered. Included there is his recollection of the afternoon of December 7, after the Japanese had departed.

Sometime later I went with a couple of other guys back to the barracks to get something to eat. The mess hall was on the first floor of our barracks and it was very large, covering most of the first floor. On this trip is when I saw the ugliest sight of the day. There had been many sailors who had either been blown into the water off the battleships or had jumped into the water to swim the short distance to Ford Island. The harbor was covered with oil from the torpedo hits and some drowned just trying to swim in the stuff. Some were wounded or burned before they entered the water. The mess hall was the natural place to take these men. When we entered the mess hall every single table had a man or a body stretched out on it. The eerie thing about it was that you could have heard a pin drop. I was more conscious of oil than I was of any blood in the scene. Some of these men were black with oil. I probably got something to eat but I don't remember it now.

Pearl Harbor Remembered. "Ted LeBaron on Ford Island." http://my.execpc.com/~dschaaf/lebaron.html.

does at the *Utah*, anchored directly behind the *Tangier*. Two torpedoes smashed into the aging battleship and created such a ferocious explosion that ladles and other hanging equipment in the *Tangier*'s galley (kitchen) flew through the air and cooks were knocked off balance. The badly hammered *Utah* sank in only eight minutes. Though other Japanese aircraft completed runs against the *Raleigh* and *Detroit*, sinking the *Raleigh* by the stern, the *Tangier* escaped harm in this first attack.

Luck and Sprague's repeated drills helped the crew of the *Tangier*, but the men received help from another source—their commander. He gave few orders, but instead trusted his men to perform their duties as expected. He quietly watched from the bridge as they executed their tasks, confident they would draw inspiration by his absolute faith in their abilities. "Sprague was always cool," explained Barnes. "At Pearl Harbor, he acted like he'd thought everything out. Sprague knew just what to do, like he was born to command during a crisis."[44]

Sprague remained on the open bridge of his ship rather in the safety of his protected bridge one deck below because he wanted the crew to see that he shared the same dangers as they did. His crew faced death for the first time, and he wanted to remain in plain sight to lend moral support at a time when it was most needed. "All those men on the main deck and above it, at one time or another as they fought," said Ensign John Hughes, "could see Sprague calmly standing there throughout the battle. That impressed us officers and encouraged the men."[45]

A confused and disordered scene developed everywhere else. Within ten minutes Kimmel had lost four battleships, and more would soon follow. "Torpedo planes swooped in from almost over my head and started toward Battleship Row," explained chief petty officer Leonard J. Fox of the scene that unfolded as he watched from the light cruiser USS *Helena*. "First the *Oklahoma* … then it was the *West Virginia* taking blows in her innards…. Now, as I looked on unbelievingly, the *California* erupted … and now it is the *Arizona*…. Men were swimming for their lives in the fire-covered waters of Pearl Harbor."[46]

Disaster at the Airfields

While sailors battled for their lives in the waters, other military personnel at the various airfields circling Pearl Harbor faced their own trials. As Japanese dive-bombers and torpedo planes rained bombs onto American ships, Fuchida's fighters beat down the U.S. air strength at the fields to deny the Americans the ability to mount a strong air counterattack. In the battle's first moments, Japanese fighter pilots blasted naval air bases at Ford Island and Kaneohe Bay, the marine fighter base at Ewa, and three army airfields at Wheeler, Bellows, and Hickam fields.

The results were the same at each location—before thirty minutes had elapsed, American air power on the island lay in ruins. Stacked closely together on the airstrips to make the planes easier to guard against sabotage, the planes formed easy targets for the skillful Japanese pilots. The naval air station at Ford Island, located in the middle of the Japanese air attacks against the battleships and other vessels anchored along the island's east and west shores, received many hits. Smoke and fire soon rose from thirty-three aircraft, mixing with the billows of black smoke coming from the damaged battleships. No American pilot even got off the ground from that location.

Twenty miles (32km) away at Kaneohe Bay along Oahu's eastern coast, the main base for land-based patrol planes and seaplanes, the Japanese pilots shot up aircraft on the field as well as ground crews and hangars. Defenders tried to mount a response, but most Japanese swept away untouched after emptying their machine guns. Private first class James Evans described his experience:

Sailors stand amidst wrecked planes at an airfield outside of Pearl Harbor as the attack continues. The Japanese attacked both the harbor and the airfields to destroy the U.S. military's response capabilities.

A couple of us took a water cooled machine gun up to the second deck of the barracks. We planned to mount the gun on the roof as we would have an excellent field of fire on the planes banking around the barracks. One of them boosted me up to the ladder leading to the roof, but when I opened the hatch and stuck my head through, here comes a Jap plane so close that I could see the pilot's teeth as he grinned at me. I'll never forget that. We made eye contact.[47]

Another Japanese pilot insulted the defenders by thumbing his nose at the Americans as his plane raced by.

At the marine air station at Ewa a few miles west of Pearl Harbor, Japanese pilots dropped as low as 20 feet (6m) above the ground to shoot the forty-nine aircraft lined up wingtip to wingtip. They completed their tasks so well that when pilots in a second attack arrived, they focused on destroying buildings and installations because so few aircraft remained undamaged. Despite the ease with which he descended on his targets, Japanese pilot Lieutenant Yoshio Shiga marveled at the courage displayed by one marine defender. The American stood in the midst of bullets and shrapnel, calmly firing his pistol at Shiga as the pilot took aim. Shiga missed the marine, but flew away convinced he had just witnessed the bravest act he had ever seen.

The Japanese easily did away with opposition at the army air base at Bellows Field, 8 miles (12.8km) south of Kaneohe Bay on Oahu's eastern coast, but the two main army air bases—Wheeler Field in the center of Oahu 10 miles (16km) north of Pearl Harbor, and Hickam Field resting along the harbor's southern shore—were able to organize a stronger answer. A Catholic chaplain had been saying an outdoor mass at Hickam when the attack began. He rushed to a nearby machine gun, carried it back to the altar, and started firing at the planes. Two army pilots, Lieutenant Kenneth Taylor and Lieutenant George Welch, managed to reach their fighters, take off, and shoot down seven Japanese aircraft in a feat that impressed the watchful Fuchida. The commander was struck that these Americans, "who, though greatly outnumbered, flew straight in to engage our planes." Even though the Americans inflicted only minor damage on the vast Japanese force, "their courage commanded the admiration and respect of our pilots."[48]

Those twelve B-17 bombers due from the mainland that trackers had originally confused with the Japanese arrived during the attack. They faced a tight predicament in landing their bombers while Japanese planes buzzed all about. The pilots braved fire from both the Japanese fighters and from American antiaircraft gunners and riflemen on the ground who shot at anything flying above. Despite the hazards, all twelve somehow landed at Hickam Field.

The sixty thousand army infantry stationed at barracks adjoining army airfields ran through enemy fire to reach their posts, many dying before they got there. "The men, oh, about 4,000 of them that were in the barracks, came boiling out some of the eight entrances to that large barracks," recalled army staff sergeant Woodrow W. Clark of the action at Hickam Field. "And as they came boiling out, the Japanese machine gunners opened up on them and mowed them down, like oats falling down, there at the doors."[49]

Not far away technical sergeant Joseph A. Pesek remained close to the barracks so he would not be caught out in the open by enemy planes, but this almost cost him his life when a bomb struck a nearby building. Pesek recalled:

It felt as though the whole hangar was lifted from the ground. The next thing I knew, I was picking myself up off the ramp between hangars 7 and 11, my back covered with white plaster blown out from the hangar. I got up and started to run again and almost made the edge of the runway when three more planes came at me. They were so low that I could see the ground kicking up where their machine-gun bullets were hitting. I hit the ground again covering my head with my hands. It seemed as though a thousand things passed through my mind, mostly of home and my family. I could not believe it when those three planes passed right over without hitting me. I looked up as they passed and thought the sky never looked bluer. I didn't even notice it at the time, but I [had torn] my fingernails down until they were bleeding, trying to make a hole in the runway, I guess.[50]

A Second Attack

A satisfied Fuchida observed the destruction below. By 8:30 A.M., thirty-five minutes after the Japanese forces had dropped the first bombs, the American fleet appeared to be little more than smoking ruins. In doing such heavy damage, Fuchida had lost only nine aircraft.

But they were not done. One hour after the opening blows, the Japanese sent a second strike against Pearl Harbor, a force of eighty-one dive-bombers, fifty-four high-level bombers, and thirty-six fighters commanded by Lieutenant Commander Shigekazu Shimazaki. From the ground seven-year-old Hawaii resident Carroll Robbins stood behind her apartment building with other tenants in Oahu when they heard a loud noise above. Someone pointed up and said, "Here

come the Japs!" Without moving a muscle, they stared as a formation of Japanese aircraft filled the sky. The spectacle, as impressive as it was frightening, caused someone to say, "My God."[51] The planes passed over so low to the ground that Robbins could clearly see the pilots' faces and their white ceremonial scarves flapping in the open cockpits.

The second group of Japanese aircraft arrived on the scene as Fuchida's first wave was departing. While the fighters kept the few American aircraft away, for an hour the bombers again struck the airfields and any ships in the harbor that had escaped damage from the first attack.

The Japanese experienced more difficulty with this second attack, though. The thick smoke billowing from wrecked battleships covered many targets. Fire rose from nearly every ship and land battery, disrupting the Japanese formations, and antiaircraft fire had so intensified that American gunners downed twenty Japanese planes. "It was not easy to pass through the concentrated antiaircraft fire," wrote Fuchida after the action. Flying so low into such thick opposition, Fuchida thought "it seemed that this might well be a date with eternity [that is, his time to die]."[52] In some places, sailors grabbed old World War I rifles, strung ammunition across their shoulders, and headed out to battle the Japanese.

Fuchida's pilots added to the destruction, however, dropping more bombs on already crippled ships and airfields. A bomb hit the battleship *Pennsylvania*, while others blasted apart the destroyers

The remains of two U.S. battleships sit in the harbor after the Japanese made two runs on Pearl Harbor during their surprise attack.

USS *Cassin* and USS *Downes* and sliced the bow off the destroyer USS *Shaw*. Aboard the *Nevada*, officers and crew hurriedly prepared to move away from its berth alongside the blazing *Arizona* and down the channel to the sea to avoid further bombs and torpedoes. Sailors draped their bodies over exposed ammunition and gunpowder to shield them from the waves of heat that glowed from the *Arizona* so they would not blow up. As the only battleship to get under way, the *Nevada* quickly drew the attention of Japanese pilots, who took aim and smashed the battleship with multiple bomb hits and many near misses. To prevent the damaged ship from sinking and blocking the harbor entrance, the *Nevada*'s captain turned the vessel out of the channel and ran the battleship aground before she reached the exit. He knew that keeping the way in and out of Pearl Harbor clear for other warships was more important than saving one aging battleship.

As the second wave departed, Fuchida circled above to survey the damage. He was both surprised and impressed at the amount of destruction his fliers had inflicted on the enemy. "I counted four battleships definitely sunk and three severely damaged, and extensive damage had also been inflicted upon other types of ships," he noted. "The seaplane base at Ford Island was all in flames, as were the airfields, especially Wheeler Field."[53]

While the American military battled for their lives at Pearl Harbor, American civilians on the mainland United States struggled with their emotions as word of the attack spread from coast to coast.

Chapter Five

Reaction and Recovery

Disbelief at the Japanese attack was not found only in the shallow waters of Pearl Harbor. As news of the incident spread around the world, people at first refused to accept that the Japanese had mysteriously sent a huge fleet of ships, somehow avoided being discovered by U.S. search planes, and then delivered a crippling blow directly against America's military fortress in the Pacific. Any such doubts soon melted away under an avalanche of information that quickly followed.

Reaction in Washington

President Franklin D. Roosevelt sat in the White House study on December 7, 1941, a tired commander in chief suddenly appearing older and wearier. The man who had breathed energy into a depressed country for much of the 1930s and brought hope to those who had little while the Great Depression raged, now struggled with his own despair.

Only moments ago he had been laughing and enjoying a light lunch in the Oval Office with his aide and close friend, Harry Hopkins, but the mood suddenly and dramatically changed at 1:40 P.M. when Roosevelt's military commanders at the huge American naval base at Pearl Harbor sent a message indicating that it was under attack. Japan, which had been expanding throughout the Pacific for almost a decade, had bombed the Hawaiian fortress and inflicted major damage to the United States Pacific Fleet. The most powerful warships of the navy that Roosevelt had loved since his youth when he had sailed the waters off New York, lay in smoldering ruins at the bottom of Pearl Harbor.

Hopkins said that the news had to be a mistake. He could not believe the Japanese could strike so quickly and with such damaging results at the most important military arsenal in the Pacific.

President Franklin Roosevelt addresses Congress about the bombing at Pearl Harbor.

But as aides rushed in and out of the office with the latest updates, Hopkins realized the news reports were not false. With each bulletin, Roosevelt's secretary, Grace Tully, noted that Roosevelt looked more nervous and tense. Every report contained fresher evidence of the disaster, causing experienced political advisers to tighten their jaws in anger and swear under their breath. When Tully handed the bulletins to Roosevelt, he repeatedly shook his head in alarm. Tully claimed that the president took the naval catastrophe

so hard that it appeared that the loss of each ship was, to him, like losing a close friend.

Hoping to gather fresher information from someone on the scene, Roosevelt contacted Hawaiian governor Joseph B. Poindexter in Honolulu. The governor of the territory of Hawaii was calmly describing the damage caused by the first air raid when he became more upset and suddenly started shouting. "My God, there's another wave of Jap planes over Hawaii right this minute,"[54] Roosevelt cried to those

Roosevelt Reacts

As President Roosevelt's personal secretary, Grace Tully, explains in her book, *F.D.R.: My Boss*, the nation's top leader and his advisers experienced the same disbelief and shock that rattled the rest of the nation.

I was rather abstractedly looking at a Sunday paper when the telephone rang and Louise Hackmeister [the White House telephone operator] said sharply: "The President wants you right away. There's a car on the way to pick you up. The Japs just bombed Pearl Harbor!" In twenty minutes I was drawing into the White House driveway, already swarming with extra police and an added detail of Secret Service men, with news and radio reporters beginning to stream into the Executive Office wing and State, War and Navy officials hurrying into the House.

At first the men around the President were incredulous; that changed to angry acceptance as new messages supported and amplified the previous ones. The Boss maintained greater outward calm than anybody else but there was rage in his very calmness. With each new message he shook his head grimly and tightened the expression of his mouth.

Within the first hour it was evident that the Navy was dangerously crippled, that the Army and Air Force were not fully prepared to guarantee safety from further shattering setbacks in the Pacific. It was easy to speculate that a Jap invasion force might be following their air strike at Hawaii—or that the West Coast itself might be marked for similar assault.

Grace Tully. *F.D.R.: My Boss*. Chicago: Peoples Book Club, 1949, p. 255.

near him. Still dizzy from hearing about the first raid, Roosevelt now had to listen helplessly as a second attack caused more confusion. He and the other men gathering in the White House could only wonder what further destruction the day might bring.

In Washington, D.C., early disbelief had turned to anger. When first informed of the attack, secretary of the navy Frank Knox said, "My God! This can't be true. This must mean the Philippines."[55] With proof arriving and additional reports of damage, however, Knox and Roosevelt turned to the business at hand. Roosevelt ordered his secretary of state, Cordell Hull, to go ahead and see the two visiting Japanese diplomats that had been scheduled to meet with him, but to say nothing of the events at Pearl Harbor.

When ambassador Kichisaburo No-mura and special envoy Saburo Kurusu walked into Hull's office to deliver the letter declaring Japan's intention to end diplomacy with the United States, they immediately sensed an icy atmosphere. U.S. codebreakers had intercepted the message earlier and had already delivered the contents to Hull. Secretary Hull received the message without looking at his guests, pretended to read the note then said with barely controlled anger that in the past nine months he had never uttered one untrue word in dealing with the Japanese. "In all my fifty years of public service," he added, "I have never seen such a document that was [so full of lies]."[56] Hull quickly sent away the puzzled diplomats.

Americans React

Much as would happen decades later on September 11, 2001, when New York's World Trade Center towers collapsed from terrorist attacks, people forever remembered where they were or what they were doing when they first learned of the Pearl Harbor attack. In New York City, radio station WOR interrupted its broadcast of the New York Giants football game to inform its audience. When the news interrupted a performance by the New York Philharmonic Orchestra, the musicians, instead of continuing with the symphony they had been playing, broke into "The Star-Spangled Banner." The concertgoers rose to their feet and, in firm voices that masked their fears, sang the anthem.

Many, knowing little about Pacific Ocean geography, wondered where

and what Pearl Harbor was. In her Los Angeles apartment Margaret Ensign was listening to the radio announcer as he described the news. She recalls, "There was a musical program on the radio, and the announcer broke in and said that the Navy had been bombed at Pearl Harbor. At first we thought it was the invasion from Mars hoax [a 1938 radio broadcast of the H.G. Wells drama "War of the Worlds," that had scared part of the country into thinking invaders from Mars had landed] all over again. When the second announcement came, Dick [her husband] and I looked at each other and said, 'Where's Pearl Harbor?'"[57]

In the San Francisco Bay area factory whistles and firehouse sirens were used as alarms to notify citizenry of any attack, while up and down the West Coast groups of city councils declared blackouts to protect vital defense plants and other locations from enemy bombings. In San Quentin Prison, ten convicts on death row volunteered to be human torpedoes against the Japanese.

Mary Joan Pinard of Prairie du Chien, Wisconsin, sat in a restaurant with friends, enjoying coffee and light talk, when someone rushed in and said, "Pearl Harbor's just been bombed." The group assumed it was a joke, but then realized the man was serious. "We all sat together and talked about what we thought were the possibilities ahead. We grew up fast—we were all seventeen, eighteen at the time."[58]

Thirteen-year-old Lucy Veltri of Racine, Wisconsin, was watching a movie at the Granada Theater in Racine when

Average net paid circulation
for September exceeded
Daily --- 1,800,000
Sunday - 3,150,000

DAILY NEWS

FINAL

NEW YORK'S PICTURE NEWSPAPER

Copyright 1938 by News Syndicate Co., Inc. Reg. U. S. Pat. Off.

Entered as 2nd class matter, Post Office, New York, N. Y.

Vol. 20. No. 109   New York, Monday, October 31, 1938★   48 Pages   2 Cents IN CITY LIMITS | 3 CENTS Elsewhere

FAKE RADIO 'WAR' STIRS TERROR THROUGH U.S.

—Story on Page 2

(NEWS foto)

"War" Victim

Caroline Cantlon, WPA actress, listening to this radio in West 49th St., heard announcement of "smoke in Times Square." Running to street, she fell, broke her arm.

(By Associated Press)

"I Didn't Know". Orson Welles, after broadcast expresses amazement at public reaction. He adapted H. G. Wells' "War of the Worlds" for radio and played principal role. Left: a machine conceived for another H. G. Wells story. Dramatic description of landing of weird "machine from Mars" started last night's panic.   —Story on page 2.

Some Americans, hearing of the Pearl Harbor attack, at first thought it was a joke, like Orson Welles' "War of the Worlds" radio broadcast.

suddenly the movie stopped and the lights came on. The manager walked to the stage and announced that Japan had bombed Pearl Harbor. "I was scared to death. It frightened me so much,"[59] Veltri remembered. Uncertain of how far Pearl Harbor was from Wisconsin, she worried that the Japanese would be in Racine at any moment.

When news of the war was announced at the Majestic Theater in Dallas, Texas, a patron brushed aside any momentary doubts and, to the cheers of those around him, said, "We'll stamp their front teeth in."[60]

Whether near or far from the attack, fear accompanied the initial news of the Japanese action. In the family apartment near Waikiki Beach in Oahu, seven-year-old Carroll Robbins and her five-year-old brother, Berton, listened to comics being read over the radio. Their attention drifted when the announcer broke the news of the bombing and began repeating that this was no drill. Their father, a navy lieutenant and the executive officer of the *Shaw*, a destroyer in drydock, burst into the room from the bedroom and shouted for Carroll to turn up the radio. He listened for a moment and then rushed out the door, shouting back to his wife to keep the radio on and not to leave the apartment.

Patriotism and anger eventually took the place of the early fear. Young men swarmed army, navy, marine, and coast guard recruiting offices, forming lines that stretched around the block. In Norfolk, Virginia, one man explained why he left home so quickly to be the first man in the recruiting line. "I want to beat them Japs with my own bare hands."[61] In Davenport, Iowa, the five Sullivan brothers enlisted in the navy together and requested that they be stationed aboard the same vessel. Sadly, within a year all five would be lost in a naval action off Guadalcanal in the South Pacific.

Anti-Japanese sentiment grew strong. *Time* magazine, which labeled the attack "premeditated murder masked by a toothy smile," stated that one question spread across the land. "What would the [American] people, the 132,000,000, say in the face of the mightiest event of their time? What they said—tens of thousands of them—was: 'Why, the yellow bastards!'"[62] One angry citizen went to the famed tidal basin in Washington, D.C., and chopped down four of the beautiful Japanese cherry trees that lined the water.

Afternoon at Pearl Harbor

While United States citizens struggled with many emotions, in Pearl Harbor sailors and officers battled to stay alive. On Battleship Row and elsewhere, wounded men continued to labor as long as possible, ignoring their wounds to help save shipmates and mount a defense against the Japanese. Crews fought on in the middle of the explosions and onrushing water, then hastily abandoned ship in attempts to save their lives. Men could not battle fires aboard the *Arizona* because they lacked pressure for the fire hoses due to bomb damage. As the crew started to leave the dying ship, men noticed a sweetish, sickening

A salvage crew stands on the tilted deck of the USS Oklahoma. *Hundreds were caught below decks when the ship capsized. Only thirty survived to be rescued.*

smell as the raging fires consumed the dead bodies of their shipmates.

Aboard the *Arizona* a thick, acrid smoke filled the area in which machinist's mate first class George D. Phraner worked, the metal walls began to get hot, and the lights went out. He and a few others made a desperate attempt to escape what was rapidly turning into a watery tomb below deck and reach the surface. "Somehow we were able to open the hatch and start to make our way up the ladder," recalled Phraner. "I was nauseated by the smell of burning flesh, which turned out to be my own as

I climbed up the hot ladder. A quick glance around revealed nothing in the darkness, but the moaning and sounds of falling bodies told me that some of my shipmates had succumbed to defeat and had died in their attempt to survive." Choking as the bitter smoke filled his lungs, Phraner became weak and lightheaded. "I could feel myself losing the battle to save my own life. I clung to the ladder, feeling good. I felt that it was all right for me to let go. At that moment I looked up and could see a small point of light through the smoke. It gave me the strength to go on."[63]

Joy in Japan

The shock and sorrow in the United States over the sudden attack against Pearl Harbor produced elation in Japan. Itabashi Koshu was a Japanese middle school student when he heard of the successful attack by his countrymen from a news bulletin announcing that war had begun.

"I felt as if my blood boiled and my flesh quivered," Koshu wrote of that December 1941 day. "The whole nation bubbled over, excited and inspired. 'We really did it! Incredible! Wonderful!' That's the way it felt then." He explained that the vast majority of his people believed Japan to be correct in launching a war. "There is a Japanese proverb that says, 'A cornered mouse will bite a cat.' America is evil, Britain is wrong, we thought. In Japan, nobody was calculating whether we would win or not. We simply hit out. Our blood was hot! We fought. No one considered the possibility that Japan could lose."

Haruko Taya Cook and Theodore F. *Cook. Japan at War: An Oral History.* New York: New Press, 1992, pp. 77–78.

Phraner later remembered that he had relied on a strength he never knew he had to reach the deck. Gasping for fresh air and glad to be alive, he looked around to witness a nightmarish scene. Flame and smoke covered much of the ship while injured men, some suffering hideous burns, wandered aimlessly about. Directly behind Phraner lay a dead marine, his body cut in two by shell shrapnel.

Phraner and others made their way to the ship's edge and entered the water. He noticed that some men removed their shoes before leaving, expecting that the weight of the footwear might make it harder to swim to shore one hundred yards away. While Phraner reached the relative safety of the beach, many of his shipmates were trapped inside the *Arizona.*

A short distance from the *Arizona*, the *West Virginia* listed so heavily that men could not walk on the slippery decks without holding on to something. Their unease was nothing compared to the decision Lieutenant Commander John S. Harper faced. Though he could plainly hear the cries of men trapped on the other side of a watertight door, begging for him to open it and save them from the rising waters, Harper could not risk endangering the rest of the ship by opening the door and permitting the water to rush into other areas. He ordered the door kept closed.

As a wall of smoke and flame advanced dangerously across the deck, men heeded the order to abandon ship. Some left in a boat from the port rail, while others leaped into the water on the starboard side. From an initial crew of 87 officers and 1,454 enlisted men, the ship lost 2 officers and 103 men killed or missing and another 52 wounded.

The *Nevada*, the only battleship able to make steam and leave her berth, presented a stirring scene to sailors on other vessels as the warship inched southward down the channel from the northernmost anchor. In the midst of the shooting and dying the ship bravely forged on, as if drawing inspiration and determination from onlookers. "The old ship fighting her way down harbor was the most inspiring sight I saw during the entire war!" said nineteen-year-old marine private first class Art Wells. "I felt pride as I watched the gallant old battlewagon slowly, determinedly, and majestically, fighting her way through rising geysers of water, shrugging off multiple bomb hits, with her guns defiantly spitting flames and projectiles at the darting planes swarming like bees above her while striving desperately to stop her."[64]

Escape from the *Oklahoma*

Experiences aboard the *Oklahoma*, while in many ways typical of what other ships endured, also offered their own dramatic twists. Naval officer Adolph D. Mortensen was trying to get above deck when the ship began sinking so quickly that he was thrown into the sick bay, trapped with only a small pocket of air in which to breathe.

Mortensen used his feet to locate an eleven-inch-wide porthole (a window-like opening) underneath the water. He ducked below the surface and opened it by hand, giving the men inside a chance to exit what was fast becoming a watery grave. "The first two men got out quickly. The ship's carpenter, Mr. Austin, a large man weighing over 200 pounds, knew he'd never make it through the porthole. He reached down and held the porthole open for me. I tried to take a deep breath, but the oxygen supply was about gone. Mr. Austin couldn't get out. His was the most noble and heroic act a man could perform, knowing full well that his minutes were few."[65] Austin, too big to get through the narrow opening, drowned while saving others.

As told by seaman first class Stephen Bower Young, the difficult situation faced by the crew of the battleship *Oklahoma* was typical of what thousands of servicemen in Pearl Harbor faced that December morning and afternoon. Men grabbed on to any solid fixture they could to keep their balance as bombs and torpedoes rocked the ship. As the water rose and the ship tilted at a dangerous angle, equipment broke loose and slid into the men. Young recounted:

Gear of all descriptions commenced [began] to tumble about, and sailors began to scramble for the ladder leading upward. I raised my head above the shell-deck level just as the *Oklahoma*'s enormous shells [bombs], weighing a ton apiece, broke loose from their moorings and rolled wildly down the slanting deck where sailors were fighting to stay on their feet. There was no possible escape for these men, and I recoiled [drew back] from the terrible sights and sounds. Sailors fell down the deck and met their deaths violently. Numbly I watched two friends of mine, arms and legs waving wildly, as they and the gear which had knocked them off their feet smashed into the debris [wreckage] at the bottom of the slanting deck. By the faint light I could see that they had joined others—floating face down in the water."[66]

As the ship began to flip over in the harbor and rest upside down on the bottom, men and debris were tossed about. Sailors struggled to break through the surface of the water, but when they did most learned that they had been trapped inside flooding compartments. One sailor swam to an escape hatch but found his way out blocked by the body of an overweight crew member wedged in the narrow opening. Confined sailors could breathe for awhile in pockets of air, but knew that as the air supply dwindled, the waters would fill more of the room. Officers among the different groups ordered men to cease talking in an effort to conserve air. Caught deep in the ship's insides, the men could now only wait with their thoughts and hope that others would come to their rescue before the air ran out. Some men waited for hours for

help to come, spending their time praying for deliverance or thinking of family and home. Young wrote:

The hours passed by. The water level rose inexorably [unstoppably], inch by awful inch. I thought of home. Days of growing up. People I had known. Long summer days of hard farm work, but with lots of time for fun. Swimming, fishing. Pleasant thoughts. Even now, in the darkness, the memories brought a smile. My family. They were a source of strength to me. It had been more than a year since I had seen them. They had all waved goodbye as I walked out of the yard that morning. How would they take the news of my death? With sadness, certainly, but with a reserved pride. I hoped they would be all right.

A sailor near Young joked gruesomely, "Join the Navy and see the world—from the bottom of Pearl Harbor."[67] To Young's surprise, the crack produced laughter and seemed to relax the group. Some placed strange bets on whether they would drown or suffocate first.

With time and air running out, men searched for other ways to escape. In some areas sailors, already short of breath, swam underneath the surface searching for hatches and portholes through which the men might escape but, apparently drowning in their attempts, were never seen again. "Suddenly, anger rumbled within me," wrote Young. "Why couldn't we have died in the sun

An Honest Mistake

Nine days after the assault on Pearl Harbor, Mr. and Mrs. Green Hamlin of Harlan, Kentucky, received a telegram from the United States Navy Department informing them that their son, twenty-seven-year old fireman first class James T. Hamlin, a sailor in the United States Navy, had been killed during the attack on December 7, 1941. The family conducted a memorial service in Harlan for the deceased sailor, and then retreated to their home to mourn the loss of their son.

Two weeks later, on New Year's Eve, the government sent a second telegram alerting them that an error had been made and that their son had survived. A difficult Christmas holiday season ended with a joyous New Year's celebration for the Hamlin family.

In the confusion attending the attack, their son had been unaware of the anguish his family had experienced.

Pearl Harbor Remembered. "Survivor James Hamlin Was Officially Killed at Pearl Harbor." http://my.execpc.com/~dschaaf/hamlin.html.

where we could have met death head on? That was the way to die, on your feet, like a man. But instead, it was to be a slow, useless death, imprisoned in our dark iron cell."[68]

In some parts of the submerged ship, many were overcome by the murky waters, dying alone or with small groups of friends. At other locations, sometimes not far from those who perished, fate smiled on other sailors as rescue crews arrived to free them from their certain death. "Unexpectedly, and from a great distance, came the sound of hammering," recalled Young. "Metal against metal! Our hearts jumped. The sound stopped, and we held our breaths. It started again, closer, and died away once more." Would rescue, a lack of oxygen, or the swirling waters reach them first? "Would we all drown like rats at the last minute, just when rescue was at hand?" he wondered. "It was going to be close, so close!"[69]

Using drills and bare hands, rescuers cut through the compartment wall to create an opening through which Young's group escaped. The men, trapped for hours below the surface and facing almost certain death, gulped fresh air as they stood on the ship's hull. Young described his emotions upon being rescued:

Standing on the upturned hull, I gazed about me. It was the same world I had left twenty-five hours before, but as I looked at the smoke and wreckage of battle, the sunken ships *Tennessee, West Virginia,* and *Arizona* astern of [behind] us, I felt that life would never be the same, not for me—not for any of us. A launch [motorboat] came alongside to take us to a hospital ship. As I stepped into the boat, I looked down at the ship we had lived in, the ship we had come so close to dying in, the tomb of friends and shipmates who were gone forever. The mighty *Oklahoma* was no more. The flag, the colored signal pennants would never fly again. Her guns were silent, her turrets [gun housings] full of men and water.[70]

In other flooded compartments inside the *Oklahoma*, desperate men continued to beat on the bulkheads as workers furiously cut through metal to reach them before their air supply gave out. "We got to the point where you could hear each other breathing," said James Bounds. "You didn't want to talk any more than you had to because

Homes and schools were also destroyed in the attack. In the aftermath, people helped one another in any way they could.

that air was getting low. It's like being in a big, black, damp, dark hole—I guess like somebody in a coffin."[71]

As the air supply thinned, the men started to lose hope. Finally, after thirty-six hours, rescue workers cut through to his bulkhead and pulled Bounds and the other men in his compartment from their watery tomb. Only thirty of four hundred men were rescued from *Oklahoma*'s insides.

Louis LaGesse, who had earlier been placed with the dead, experienced a resurrection. Believed to be a dead sailor, he was transported to a boat for taking to a burial ceremony. The man who carried him, however, noticed LaGesse's eyelashes move slightly. Instead of the burial service, the man moved LaGesse to a hospital ship and treatment.

Events Elsewhere

The men aboard the navy's battleships were not the only ones experiencing an arduous day. Early in the attack the destroyer USS *Monaghan* sighted one of the five Japanese midget submarines sent to create a disturbance inside the harbor, rammed it, dropped depth charges, and sank the boat. The skipper of another midget submarine beached his craft because of severe damage, and the other three disappeared somewhere in the waters off Hawaii. The five played no major role in the action.

Military personnel and civilians alike faced situations they could never have imagined only twenty-four hours earlier. Seaman D.F. Calkins received orders to investigate the remains of a Japanese aircraft that had been shot down. When he approached the plane, rifle at the ready, he spotted the Japanese pilot sitting on the wing. Calkins shouted for the man to surrender, but had to shoot when the Japanese airman refused to surrender and reached for his pistol.

Women performed bravely as well. After her serviceman husband left to report to duty, island resident Johnie Gano picked up two of her friends, one of whom had an eleven-month-old child, and drove to a large deserted canal in the hills that had been designated as a safe area. A guard stood watch in case Japanese ground forces invaded Oahu, but after three days the group was sent back home when it became clear that the threat of invasion had passed.

Other women helped tend the wounded and dying. Along with neighbors and friends, Betty Garrett evacuated her home and found safety in a bachelor officers' building. They at first intended to wait out events, but when a stream of exhausted, wounded men poured in from the harbor area, Garrett and others pitched in to help. They searched the building for unused cots and clothing, as many of the weary sailors had lost shirts and slacks in swimming away from sinking ships, and carted out a supply of candy bars and cigarettes for the men. She recalled:

And then they started coming—by the hundreds and in all stages of undress. As the ships exploded, their fuel oil spread over the water, and men who were not thrown into the harbor by the force of the explosions had no choice but to jump overboard and swim to shore. When they reached the island they were covered with oil.

Eyes—big white eyes—stared out of blackened faces. We were seeing the uninjured and the less severely injured, those who could swim to shore and still walk to the bachelors' quarters. Often we had to light their cigarettes for them— their hands shook too violently to hold the match. For some we also held the cup of water.[72]

Red Cross volunteer Evelyn Guthrie faced worse conditions at her station adjoining the harbor, where she tended wounded men at Tripler Army Hospital while the fighting raged. "A scene of unbelievable horror greeted us," she said of the events she first viewed after arriving at the hospital. "Several of the battleships were afire. Men were jumping overboard and trying to swim through the fiery oil on the surface of the water. I confess that I felt tears streaming down my face at this nightmarish spectacle [scene]. But there was no time for tears or thoughts." As a line of ambulances brought in a seemingly endless number of bloody, torn men, the small collection of overwhelmed doctors and nurses at Tripler did what they could, but they were limited by having only a small staff. Many physicians and nurses were unable to get to the hospital in the day's confusion, and as a result some wounded men died who might have normally survived.

"All of those who had lost an arm or a leg died that day,"[73] explained Guthrie.

As a volunteer she lacked the training possessed by regular nurses, and often found herself simply holding the hands of dying men to bring small comfort to their final moments. Nearby, a hospital orderly held back tears as he mopped blood from the floor so no one would slip. Once he finished cleaning the room, he had to start again, as more wounded and dying had been brought in.

The day affected children as profoundly as it did adults. Seven-year-old Carroll Robbins was not afraid, she later recalled, until someone told her about a resident who had been killed while walking across street. The young girl also noticed missing chunks from buildings and other debris that littered the area, and did not know what to think when adults near her, the people she relied upon to protect her and her brother, became hysterical and screamed uncontrollably. Her concerns grew when a soldier said that the island would be placed under martial law. The girl had no idea that the word "martial" referred to the military taking command over Oahu. Unfamiliar with its meaning, all Carroll knew was the word sounded alarming. Increasing her fears was the fact that she still had no idea whether her father was alive or dead.

Everyone, it seemed, had to adjust to a new situation that December 7. Everything had changed in a few spectacular, deadly moments of a morning that shook the foundations of a nation and left so-called normal routines in pieces.

Chapter Six

Aftermath

At dusk on December 8, from the deck of the aircraft carrier USS *Enterprise,* vice admiral William F. Halsey, commander of the aircraft battle force, led the ships in his task force into Pearl Harbor. The force had been at sea during the attack, and Halsey braced for what he guessed would be a scene of alarming destruction. Flames consumed ships and buildings, while billowing black smoke hung over every area. The hulls of Halsey's ships brushed aside debris in the narrow channel as they moved toward their berths. The odor of burning oil and bodies sickened some of the crew that stood along the edge of the flight deck, while the sights, sounds, and smells moved many to tears. The battleship *Nevada* lay grounded by the stern, and water swept across the decks of its fellow battlewagon, the *California,* which had settled to the bottom. In the spot where the *Enterprise* would have berthed had she arrived as originally scheduled, the battleship *Utah* lay belly-up in the water. Halsey quietly surveyed the damage, taking in the incredible destruction, then cursed through clenched teeth, "Before we're through with 'em, the Japanese language will be spoken only in hell!"[74]

A lieutenant commander aboard the *Enterprise* said, "Passing Battleship Row was the saddest sight any seaman has ever seen. The first ship I sighted was the *Nevada,* down by the stern. Battleship Row was lying on its heels. The *California* was down, her decks awash. It looked as though all the battleships on the outboard side had been sunk, while those inboard were saved because of this outboard ship protection. The sight of this destruction none of us on the *Enterprise* can ever forget."[75]

Measuring the Destruction at Pearl Harbor

Hundreds of soldiers manning their posts at Pearl Harbor watched the *Enterprise* and her escorts return. Some, still numb

Mitsuo Fuchida served as flight commander of the Japanese attack on Pearl Harbor. He urged a third attack, but Admiral Nagumo did not agree.

from the fighting, stared without muttering a sound. With nothing but damaged battleships and cruisers scattered about the harbor, the soldiers decided they had to place their hopes in what was left. As one army officer told his navy friend, "It's up to you carrier boys now. Pearl Harbor must be held, and you're all we've got left in the Pacific!"[76]

In the two waves, the Japanese destroyed 188 aircraft and damaged another 159, most before they even left the ground. The Japanese sank or damaged 21 ships, most in the battle's opening fifteen minutes, including 7 battleships. The explosions and bullets killed 2,403 Americans, including 1,177 crewmen aboard the *Arizona* alone and 68 civilians, and wounded another 1,178. The navy lost three times as many men at Pearl Harbor as it had lost in the Spanish-American War of 1898 and World War I combined. Only 29 Japanese aircraft and pilots were lost, and 5 midget subs and one large submarine destroyed.

"We witnessed total destruction of houses in the Pearl City area, and knew children must have lived in them as bent and burned remnants of toys were scattered in the debris," remembered Carroll Robbins. "We saw trucks reduced to flattened metal, almost unrecognizable, and a car riddled with bullet holes still containing several dead bodies. The smell of burning oil was pungent [sharp] and hung in the air for a long time."[77]

Robert J. Casey, a newspaper reporter observing the events, decided that the Japanese could not have wasted many shots in light of all the destruction he witnessed, which he called "startling, stupendous, and disgraceful." The images created the nightmare scene of an enemy free to roam the Pacific while the United States stood helplessly by. "You got the impression that whatever the inventory [list] of damage, the United States wasn't going to hit back because the United States couldn't hit back." He added, "We began to wonder, as many a person was wondering in Honolulu right at that time, if we weren't [adding] up the score for a war that had ended before it began."[78]

As terrible as the attack was, it could have been worse. Yamamoto had hoped to catch the valuable American aircraft carriers at anchor, but all three had been out on missions. The USS *Saratoga* steamed off California, while the USS *Lexington* and the *Enterprise* delivered aircraft to Wake Island and Midway. Had the Japanese destroyed even two of these three, they would have solidified their hold in the Pacific to such an extent that Roosevelt might have seriously considered asking for a cease-fire.

When Fuchida returned to the carrier *Akagi*, he urged Admiral Nagumo to launch a third strike to destroy the installations that had not been touched, including the fuel and torpedo storage areas and the repair facilities that kept the remaining ships going while the nation regrouped. Without those assets, the U.S. Navy may very well have had to pull back to California, a move that would have yielded Pacific domination to the Japanese and could have lengthened the war.

Winston Churchill's Response to the Attack

One Allied leader who found a ray of hope in the Pearl Harbor attack was British prime minister Winston Churchill. As related by John Costello in his book *The Pacific War, 1941–1945*, when he first learned of the assault, like many others he reacted with stunned surprise. "Mr. President, what's all this about Japan?" he asked in his first call to the American leader. Roosevelt confirmed that the fighting had begun. "They have attacked Pearl Harbor," he told Churchill. "We are all in the same boat now."

Churchill detested the destruction and death caused by the Japanese, but he now had the most powerful nation in the world actively on his side. For two years he had battled Hitler's legions, often alone, but he could now count on America to help him finish the task. For the first time in many months, Winston Churchill thought that victory lay within the Allies' grasp and went to bed and slept "the sleep of the saved and the thankful."

John Costello. *The Pacific War 1941–1945*. New York: Quill Books, 1982, pp. 141, 148.

Nagumo dismissed Fuchida's arguments. He believed that the missing American aircraft carriers lurked in the vicinity, that American defenses at Pearl Harbor would be waiting for his aircraft to appear and would thus shoot down a large number, and he was not about to tempt fate by staying too long within range of American land-based aircraft. He ordered the force to head back to Japan.

With its battleships largely in ruins, the U.S. Navy had no choice but to turn to the weapons it still possessed—its aircraft carriers and submarines. In the war's opening months those vessels kept the Japanese off balance and prevented further advances. Then, supported by hundreds of other ships that poured out of American shipyards in the next few years, they anchored the successful four-year drive across the Pacific Ocean that resulted in final victory in 1945. Nagumo made a serious mistake in not ordering a third strike against Pearl Harbor.

"Only that Providence which seems to watch over fools and sailors had saved our navy from an even worse disaster," wrote Foster Hailey of the *New York Times*, who witnessed much of the war's early action. "No nation ever went to war, or rather was pitchforked [thrown] into war, as poorly prepared as was the United States in the Pacific."[79] Hailey claimed that the nation should have considered it a blessing that the Japanese did not go on to attack the West Coast as well.

Repair and Recovery

Survivors at Pearl Harbor worked around the clock to rescue trapped sailors and raise sunken ships. Twenty-year-old seaman first class Glen Turner of the *California* saw many horrible scenes during those days but considered the worst to be going back on board his battleship to retrieve the bodies of his shipmates, many burned beyond recognition or ripped into pieces.

Military crews repaired all but three of the ships sunk or damaged at Pearl Harbor. The *Oklahoma* was raised from the waters but was considered too badly damaged to be saved, while the aging *Utah*, used primarily as a training ship, was left untouched. The *Arizona*, containing the bodies of more than a thousand servicemen, to this day remains submerged in the harbor waters, resting as a memorial to that fateful day. The rest were either patched up in Hawaii and rejoined the fleet or refloated and sent to mainland shipyards for repairs.

Lingering Fears in Hawaii

Meanwhile, reaction in the Hawaiian Islands ranged from disbelief to panic about the possibility of a Japanese invasion of the United States. One soldier stated that there was no way the U.S. forces could deter a Japanese invasion, even if the enemy landed in canoes. Reports of supposed sightings flooded military communications centers—a ship was seen off the coast here, an enemy submarine there, saboteurs everywhere. Spies, according to mistaken reports, cut large arrows in sugarcane fields directing Fuchida's aircraft to the right locations, and sympathetic Hawaiians of Japanese ancestry were prepared to join in overthrowing the island's government. The Hawaiians' fears intensified when the December 8 issue of the *Honolulu Advertiser* declared in its headline that saboteurs had already landed.

Peggy Hughes Ryan, the wife of a navy officer, heard rumors that Japanese carriers prowled not far offshore and that enemy parachutists had dropped onto the island. When the child of one of her friends cried, the mother calmed her by claiming she would use their father's navy dress sword to keep any Japanese soldiers from harming them. Residents, fully expecting an invasion, expressed their fears to war reporter Robert Casey that their military now lacked the ability to do much about it. One woman remarked to Casey that the United States would have to fall back to the mountains of the Sierra Nevada in California until the country could rebuild a new navy.

Authorities placed a curfew on civilian households, which made it illegal to go out after a certain time, and few dared to leave their homes after dark. As frightened as residents were, people shot at anything moving about in the dark. Six fighter aircraft from the *Enterprise* approached Ford Island the night of December 7, and despite word being sent that the planes were friendly, nervous gun crews and guards peppered the aircraft with bullets, killing three of the pilots.

At least Carroll Robbins breathed easier about her father. After laboring through the day on his destroyer, he

Time Magazine Reflects on the Onset of War

Time magazine was the nation's most influential newsmagazine at the time of the attack on Pearl Harbor. As it often did, the magazine reflected the mood of the nation after the attack, which was negative, to say the least. Those emotions clearly emerged in the December 15 and December 22 issues, the first two to appear on newsstands after the attack.

"What the hell was the Navy doing out there?" asked Topeka, Kansas, inhabitants of a *Time* reporter. When the Kansans expressed their hopes for a speedy response, the reporter noted that "underneath there is a vein of anxiety and determination, a sag in optimism. . . ."

The magazine noted, however, that the country would have to wait for a meaningful response from a hamstrung military. "Like a boxer who is slammed before he can get off his stool, the Pacific Fleet had first to get itself up. From that time until the day when it can report its first victories over the Japanese, its role is primarily defensive." The magazine concluded that in light of the drastic circumstances "a revolutionary strategy" was required of the military. "When Japanese bombers whipped over the frowning fastness of Diamond Head last Sunday morning the book of traditional U.S. naval strategy in the Pacific was torn to shreds."

"Lifeline Cut." *Time*, December 15, 1941, p. 24; "Great Change," December 22, 1941, p. 11.

---

returned home for a few hours, carrying with him the bullet-riddled flag from the *Shaw*.

A Nation Officially at War

At 8:40 P.M. December 7 in Washington, D.C., top political advisers entered President Roosevelt's study in the White House to be told about the day's events. Most had been out of town on business and had been quickly called back to Washington by White House operators, so they knew little of the day's events. When labor secretary Frances Perkins arrived, she noticed that the president's usual warm greeting had been replaced with a brief hello.

Roosevelt started by labeling the meeting the most serious Cabinet session since Abraham Lincoln assembled his advisers in the dark, early days of the Civil War. In a subdued voice Roosevelt explained that the nation had taken serious losses and that the navy had suffered the worst defeat in its history. Perkins later described the scene:

His pride in the Navy was so terrific that he was having actual physical difficulty in getting out the words that put him on record as knowing that the Navy was caught unawares, that bombs dropped on ships that were not in fighting shape and not prepared to move, but were just tied up. I remember that he said twice to [secretary of the navy W. Franklin] Knox, "Find out, for God's sake, why those ships were tied up in rows."

Perkins later added, "It was obvious to me that Roosevelt was having a dreadful time just accepting the idea that the Navy could be caught unawares."[80]

People in all corners of the nation wondered what had happened as the day unfolded. Their faith in the ability of their military to keep them out of harm's way had been badly shaken, so much so that one of the most respected publications of the country, *Time* magazine, bluntly stated, "The U.S. Navy was caught with its pants down. Within one tragic hour—before the war had really begun—the U.S. appeared to have suffered greater naval losses than in the whole of World War I."[81]

Fear and uncertainty produced rumors that made already nervous citizens more likely to panic. Reports circulated that a group of Japanese aircraft had flown over San Jose, California. The mayor of Seattle, Washington, expecting a Japanese air attack, turned his office into a twenty-four-hour command center and remained there, catching a few moments of sleep whenever he could. Some politicians urged the president to consider the West Coast unable to be

defended and to pull back the military to fortified positions in the Rocky Mountains; workers piled sandbags on Washington, D.C., sidewalks, and soldiers with bayoneted rifles guarded the doors to public buildings. New York City tracked what they labeled a suspicious aircraft. A taxi driver, taking a newspaper reporter to his destination, wondered if German dictator Adolf Hitler would try to send aircraft to bomb the United States. Journalist Hanson Baldwin wrote in the *New York Times* that the coming struggle was a war the nation could well lose. Roosevelt's son Elliott even called him from Texas to explain that he had heard the Japanese were about to launch an attack from Mexico against Texas or California.

That evening Roosevelt called his secretary, Grace Tully, into his study to dictate the words he intended to use to Congress the next day in asking for a declaration of war. "Sit down, Grace," the president said to Tully. "I'm going before Congress tomorrow. I'd like to dictate my message. It will be short."[82]

Tully recalled that Roosevelt spoke clearly and calmly, precisely saying each word as if a single misspoken word might wreck the entire speech. He even dictated each punctuation mark to make sure Tully correctly typed the draft he would use.

On December 8 President Roosevelt walked to the speaker's platform of the House of Representatives to ask Congress to declare war on Japan. The president, who used a wheelchair in private, preferred to walk into the room, and leaned

LATEST
WALL ST.
PRICES
Real Estate, Page 31
PRICE THREE CENTS

New York World-Telegram

Copyright, 1941, by New York World-Telegram Corporation. All rights reserved.

Local Forecast: Light rains tonight, somewhat higher temperatures than last night; tomorrow cloudy followed by clearing, cooler than today.

VOL. 74.—NO. 135.—IN TWO SECTIONS—SECTION ONE   NEW YORK, MONDAY, DECEMBER 8, 1941.   Entered as second class matter Post Office, New York, N. Y.

1500 DEAD IN HAWAII
CONGRESS VOTES WAR

Tally in Senate Is 82 to 0, In House 388 to 1, with Miss Rankin Sole Objector

By LYLE C. WILSON,
United Press Staff Correspondent.

WASHINGTON, Dec. 8.—Congress today proclaimed existence of a state of war between the United States and the Japanese Empire 33 minutes after President Roosevelt stood before a joint session to ask such action and pledge that we will triumph—"so help us, God."

Democracy was proving its right to a place in the

100 to 200 Soldiers Killed in Japanese Raid On Luzon in Philippines

By the United Press.

BULLETIN.

MANILA, Dec. 8.—Press dispatches reported that 100 to 200 troops, 60 of them Americans, were killed or injured today when Japanese warplanes raided Iba, on the west coast of the island of Luzon, north of the Olangapo naval base.

BULLETIN.

The Japanese attack on Pearl Harbor was an act of war. On December 8, Congress declared war, and the United States entered World War II.

for support on the arms of his son marine captain James Roosevelt. With him were his wife, Eleanor, and Mrs. Woodrow Wilson, whose husband had once appeared before Congress to ask for a similar declaration for World War I.

In calm, steady tones, the president began his speech to the hushed crowd. "Yesterday, December 7, 1941—a date which will live in infamy [disgrace]—the United States of America was suddenly and deliberately attacked by naval and air forces of the Empire of Japan."

Roosevelt then warned Japan that the American people, stunned as they were, would never forget such a monstrous deed. "With confidence in our armed

forces—with the unbounding determination of our people—we will gain the inevitable triumph—so help us God."[83]

When Congress overwhelmingly passed the resolution, the United States was officially at war with Japan. Three days later, when both Germany and Italy declared war on the United States in support of their ally, Japan, the country faced a war fought in Europe, Asia, and the Pacific. A world war had truly been placed at the country's doorstep.

Angry Reaction

At a press conference with reporters the day following his speech to Congress, Roosevelt continued his efforts to be honest in how he summed up the situation, while at the same time encouraging the people. He warned that hard times lay ahead and asked the country to unite in a grand effort to defeat the enemy.

> We are now in this war. We are all in it—all the way. Every single man, woman, and child is a partner in the most tremendous undertaking of our American history. We must share together the bad news and the good news, the defeats and the victories—the changing fortunes of war.
>
> So far, the news has been all bad. We have suffered a serious set-back in Hawaii. Our forces in the Philippines, which include the brave people of that Commonwealth, are taking punishment, but are vigorously defending themselves. The reports from Guam and Wake and Midway Islands are still confused, but we must be prepared for the announcement that all these three outposts have been seized.[84]

Actions Against Japanese Americans

While Roosevelt rallied the nation and its armed forces from the worst military disaster in memory, life for citizens of Japanese ancestry in Hawaii and the West Coast grew tense as citizens in Hawaii and the mainland vented their anger against them. Two days after the attack, marine first lieutenant Cornelius C. Smith Jr. received orders to search the homes of Japanese Americans on Oahu to check for radio equipment or other signs of spying. Smith did not hesitate to follow the orders as he, like many of his compatriots, was suspicious of Japanese Americans on the island who still wore traditional Japanese clothing; hung pictures on their walls of the Japanese emperor, Hirohito; and attended Japanese-speaking schools. Similar actions occurred on the mainland. Throughout the night of December 7–8 the Seattle, Washington, police rounded up fifty-one Japanese suspected of aiding the enemy.

Emotions rose in response to testimony given during investigations of the Pearl Harbor attack. Admiral Kimmel and General Short agreed that the Japanese had amazingly accurate information on ships and procedures at the Hawaiian base, material that could, in their opinion, only have come from spies operating on Oahu. Angus M. Taylor, the United States attorney for Hawaii, pointed to an event on the Hawaiian island of Niihau as proof that Americans of Japanese ancestry would support the enemy. During the Pearl Harbor attack, when the pilot of a damaged Japanese aircraft landed on Niihau, residents of Japanese ancestry aided the man.

In the climate of fear and suspicion that existed following Pearl Harbor, citizens living along the West Coast were especially concerned about possible violent actions by the large group of Japanese Americans who lived in the region. Many of the Japanese Americans had been born in the United States and

Japanese Americans stand behind fencing at an internment camp in California. In the aftermath of the attack on Pearl Harbor, Japanese Americans were forced to relocate to internment camps for the length of the war.

felt little connection to Japan, but in light of what had happened in the Pacific, West Coast residents no longer trusted their Japanese American neighbors. California governor Culbert L. Olson said to the press that most Californians believed that they lived in the midst of enemies and that no one trusted Japanese Americans.

The people of the West Coast felt vulnerable to Japanese attack. By December 9, eleven aircraft and thirty-eight Japanese naval vessels approaching from the ocean had reportedly threatened Los Angeles. The aircraft were confirmed as false alarms. and the ships proved to be nothing more than American fishing boats operating off the coast, but other events proved more threatening. During one December week, nine Japanese submarines attacked eight American merchant ships off the California coast, sinking two and damaging two while killing six seamen. One submarine, the *I-10*, had taken up position off San Diego.

Learn from the Past

Marine first lieutenant Cornelius C. Smith Jr. maintained a diary in the aftermath of the Pearl Harbor attacks. In his entry for December 17, he records his thoughts on that epochal day. His words in 1941 carry a relevant meaning and warning for educators and students today. Smith wrote, "A new slogan is seen everywhere: 'Remember Pearl Harbor!' It has a ring about it like, 'Remember the Alamo!' [from the War for Texas Independence in 1836] or 'Remember the *Maine*! [from the Spanish-American War of 1898].' I guess that years from now kids will see it in history books, and maybe some kid will raise his hand wildly, wanting to tell how his grandfather shot down a Jap plane, or got wounded, or caught a spy. And the teacher may be an unimaginative soul who will shut the kid up—but that all belongs to another day."

As quoted in Colonel Cornelius C. Smith Jr., ". . . A Hell of a Christmas," in Paul Stilwell, ed., *Air Raid: Pearl Harbor!* Annapolis, MD: Naval Institute Press, 1981. pp. 225–226.

Concerned organizers changed the site of the 1942 Rose Bowl from its traditional home at Pasadena, California, to Durham, North Carolina, near the nation's eastern coast. The country's attorney general cautioned people not to underestimate Japan's ability to strike at the mainland, and even the president took a gloomy view. When asked at a press conference whether he could guarantee that Japan would not attack Alaska or the West Coast, Roosevelt replied he could not. "Enemy bombers could bomb Sacramento tomorrow night,"[85] he admitted.

With unrest growing, on February 19, 1942, President Roosevelt signed Executive Order No. 9066, handing the War Department the authority to designate certain areas as military zones and the power to remove any person from those areas. Though outwardly an order meant for the entire nation, the president's order targeted one group—the 127,000 Japanese Americans who lived along the West Coast. By September more than 100,000 Japanese Americans had been forced to leave their homes and businesses and move to ten permanent camps at isolated inland sites.

American citizens of Japanese ancestry were not the only individuals to feel the results of the attack on Pearl Harbor. After such a disaster, the nation needed to vent its wrath on someone. Despite the officers' arguments that they had never received sufficient information alerting them to the possibility of a Japanese attack, eight Congressional investigations and Naval Board of Inquiry hearings laid blame for the tragedy at the feet of Admiral Kimmel and General Short, both of whom were relieved of their commands. Kimmel wrote his memoirs in 1955 to defend his actions, but the debate over who was most responsible—Kimmel, Short, President Roosevelt, the nation's military—has never been satisfactorily resolved.

Americans Unite

The United States faced an almost impossible task. Yamamoto had removed the only instrument that could have stopped his nation's aggression—the United States Navy—and the Japanese prepared to deliver more blows to Allied forces throughout the Pacific. The United States had to hold on long enough for her military and industrial machines to start producing the weapons of war in massive numbers.

Made bold by their triumph at Pearl Harbor, the Japanese military unleashed other operations throughout Asia and the Pacific. Certain they had stopped the Americans from being able to wage war, Japanese commanders became overconfident and fell victim to what some historians labeled as victory disease. An belief that they could easily roll over American forces in any following operations led to a lack of effort, a weakness

the United States took advantage of in future clashes. Before 1942 had ended, American naval and land forces had inflicted defeats on the Japanese navy in the Coral Sea near Australia and off Midway Island in the central Pacific and had begun driving out the Japanese army from Guadalcanal in the South Pacific.

Despite inflicting severe harm to the United States Navy and gaining Pacific supremacy for a time with his Pearl Harbor attack, Admiral Yamamoto had overlooked one crucial factor—he had not counted on the impact of the surprise attack on the American people. Men and women rallied to the cry, "Remember Pearl Harbor" and recruiting stations had their fill of applicants for service in the nation's military. "The main flaw in the strategy of the Japanese," wrote newspaper reporter Foster Hailey, "was that they overestimated their own strength and underestimated the productive ability of the United States industry and the fighting ability of the 'soft' American man."[86]

The smoking wreckage at Pearl Harbor fueled a newfound determination. Made stronger by the weapons and machinery that soon began pouring from U.S. factories, Americans united in a wholehearted commitment to victory in World War II.

Notes

Introduction: Surprise Attack

1. Author interview with Leonard Barnes, seaman first class aboard the USS *Tangier*, April 4, 1992.

Chapter One: Opening Act of World War II

2. Charles Bracelen Flood. *Hitler: The Path to Power*. Boston: Houghton Mifflin, 1989, pp. 91–92.
3. Quoted in William E. Leuchtenburg, *The Perils of Prosperity, 1914–1932*. Chicago: University of Chicago Press, 1958, pp. 13–14
4. William L. Shirer. *Berlin Diary*. New York: Knopf, 1941, pp. 51–52.
5. Quoted in Winston S. Churchill, *The Gathering Storm*. Boston: Houghton Mifflin, 1948, p. 318.
6. Quoted in John Costello, *The Pacific War 1941–1945*. New York: Quill Books, 1982, p. 71.

Chapter Two: The United States Moves Toward War

7. Quoted in Ronald H. Spector, *Eagle Against the Sun*. New York: Free Press, 1985, p. 2.
8. Quoted in Walter Lord, *Day of Infamy*. New York: Henry Holt, 1957, p. 8.
9. Quoted in John Toland, *But Not in Shame*. New York: Random House, 1961, p. 6.

10. Quoted in Lord, *Day of Infamy*, p. 12.
11. Quoted in Costello, *The Pacific War*, p. 82.
12. Quoted in Costello, *The Pacific War*, p. 122.
13. Quoted in Toland, *But Not in Shame*, p. 5.
14. "Battle Stations." *Time*, December 8, 1941, p. 15.

Chapter Three: The Attack Opens

15. Quoted in Paul Stilwell, ed. *Air Raid: Pearl Harbor!* Annapolis, MD: Naval Institute Press, 1981, p. 2.
16. Quoted in Stilwell, *Air Raid: Pearl Harbor!*, p. 6.
17. Quoted in Samuel Eliot Morison, *History of the United States Naval Operations in World War II*, vol. 3: *The Rising Sun in the Pacific, 1931–April 1942*. Boston: Little, Brown, 1965, p. 89.
18. Quoted in Stilwell, *Air Raid: Pearl Harbor!*, p. 8.
19. Quoted in Costello, *The Pacific War, 1941–1945*, p. 124.
20. Quoted in Lord, *Day of Infamy*, pp. 6–7.
21. Quoted in Stilwell, *Air Raid: Pearl Harbor!*, p. 9.
22. Mitsuo Fuchida and Masatake Okumiya. *Midway: The Battle That*

Doomed Japan. Annapolis, MD: Naval Institute Press, 1955, p. 27.

23. Quoted in Morison, *The Rising Sun in the Pacific,* pp. 94–95.

24. Quoted in Lord, *Day of Infamy,* p. 83.

25. John E. Lacouture. "Oral History of the Pearl Harbor Attack, 7 December 1941." www.history.navy.mil/faqs/faq66-3d.htm.

26. Quoted in Lord, *Day of Infamy,* p. 145.

27. Quoted in Morison, *The Rising Sun in the Pacific,* p. 101.

28. Art Wells. "A Marine at Pearl Harbor." Pearl Harbor Remembered. http://my.execpc.com/~dschaaf/wells.html.

29. Stephen Bower Young. "God, Please Get Us Out of This," *American Heritage,* April 1966. www.americanheritage.com/articles/magazine/ah/1966/3/1966_3_48.shtml.

30. Quoted in Toland, *But Not in Shame,* p. 27.

31. Joseph A. Pesek. "Tech. Sgt Pesek Runs for His Life At Hickam." Pearl Harbor Remembered. http://my.execpc.com/~dschaaf/pesek.html.

32. Quoted in Lord, *Day of Infamy,* p. 85.

Chapter Four: The Agony of Battleship Row

33. Quoted in Stilwell, *Air Raid: Pearl Harbor!,* p. 14.

34. Quoted in Flashback Television Limited, *Pacific: The Lost Evidence, Pearl Harbour,* television documentary, 2005.

35. Quoted in Selected Naval Documents: World War II, Department of Navy, Naval History and Heritage Command, "Reports by Survivors of Pearl Harbor Attack." www.history. navy.mil/docs/wwii/pearl/survivors2.htm.

36. George D. Phraner. "George Phraner's Brush with Death Aboard the U.S.S. *Arizona,*" Pearl Harbor Remembered. http://my.execpc.com/~dschaaf/phraner.html.

37. Quoted in Flashback Television Limited, *Pacific: The Lost Evidence, Pearl Harbour.*

38. Statement of Lt. Commander T.T. Beattie. U.S. Navy, Navigator, USS *West Virginia,* in "Action of December 7, 1941—Report of December 11," 1941, p. 9.

39. Quoted in Stilwell, *Air Raid: Pearl Harbor!,* p. 13.

40. Quoted in Flashback Television Limited, *Pacific: The Lost Evidence, Pearl Harbour.*

41. Statement of Commander Jesse L. Kenworthy Jr. U.S. Navy, "Surprise Enemy Attack and Sinking of the U.S.S. *Oklahoma,* December 16, 1941," in *U.S.S.* Oklahoma *Action Report,* December 18, 1941, p. 3.

42. Quoted in Flashback Television Limited, *Pacific: The Lost Evidence, Pearl Harbour.*

43. Author's interview with Leonard Barnes, April 4, 1992.

44. Barnes interview.

45. Author's interview with John Hughes, ensign aboard the USS *Tangier,* April 24, 1992.

46. Quoted in Dan van der Vat, *The Pacific Campaign.* New York: Simon & Schuster, 1991, p. 21.

47. James Evans. "A Kanehoe Naval Air Station Remembrance," Pearl Harbor Remembered. http://my.execpc.com/~dschaaf/evans.html.

48. Quoted in Stilwell, *Air Raid: Pearl Harbor!*, p. 15.

49. Woodrow W. Clark. "Woodrow Clark Was at Hickam Field," Pearl Harbor Remembered. http://my.execpc.com/~dschaaf/w_clark.html.

50. Joseph A. Pesek. "Tech. Sgt Pesek Runs for His Life At Hickam," Pearl Harbor Remembered. http://my.execpc.com/~dschaaf/pesek.html.

51. Wilbur D. Jones Jr. and Carroll Robbins Jones. *Hawaii Goes to War*. Shippensburg, PA: White Mane Books, 2001, p. xii.

52. Quoted in Stilwell, *Air Raid: Pearl Harbor!*, p. 11.

53. Quoted in Costello, *The Pacific War*, p. 140.

Chapter Five: Reaction and Recovery

54. Quoted in Grace Tully, *F.D.R.: My Boss*. Chicago: Peoples Book Club, 1949, p. 255.

55. Quoted in Costello, *The Pacific War*, p. 138.

56. Quoted in Toland, *But Not in Shame*, p. 36.

57. Quoted in Don DeNevi, *The West Coast Goes to War, 1941–1942*. Missoula, MT: Pictorial Histories, 1998, p. 13.

58. Quoted in Michael E. Stevens, ed. *Women Remember the War, 1941–1945*. Madison: State Historical Society of Wisconsin, 1993, p. 4.

59. Quoted in Stevens, *Women Remember the War*, p. 6.

60. Quoted in *Time*, "What People Said," December 15, 1941, p. 17.

61. Quoted in *Time*, "What People Said," p. 17.

62. Quoted in *Time*, "What People Said," p. 17.

63. Phraner. "George Phraner's Brush with Death Aboard the U.S.S. Arizona."

64. Art Wells. "A Marine at Pearl Harbor," Pearl Harbor Remembered. http://my.execpc.com/~dschaaf/wells.html.

65. Adolph D. Mortensen. "Adolph Mortensen Remembers His Escape from the U.S.S. *Oklahoma*," Pearl Harbor Remembered. http://my.execpc.com/~dschaaf/morten.html.

66. Young, "God, Please Get Us Out of This," p. 2.

67. Young, "God, Please Get Us Out of This," p. 4.

68. Young, "God, Please Get Us Out of This," p. 5.

69. Young, "God, Please Get Us Out of This," pp. 5–6.

70. Young, "God, Please Get Us Out of This," p. 6.

71. Quoted in Flashback Television Limited, *Pacific: The Lost Evidence, Pearl Harbour*.

72. Betty Garrett. "A Date with a Bombing," *American Heritage*, December 1991. www.americanheritage.com/articles/magazine/ah/1991/8/1991_8_36.shtml.

73. Quoted in Stilwell, *Air Raid: Pearl Harbor!*, pp. 239–41.

Chapter Six: Aftermath

74. William F. Halsey and J. Bryan III. *Admiral Halsey's Story*. New York: McGraw-Hill, 1947, p. 81.

75. Quoted in Eugene Burns, *Then There Was One*. New York: Harcourt, Brace, 1944, p. 17.

76. Quoted in Burns, *Then There Was One*, p. 17.

77. Jones and Jones, *Hawaii Goes to War*, pp. 1–2.

78. Robert Casey. *Torpedo Junction: With the Pacific Fleet from Pearl Harbor to Midway*. New York: Bobbs-Merrill, 1942, pp. 24–25.

79. Foster Hailey. *Pacific Battle Line*. New York: Macmillan, 1944, p. 5.

80. Quoted in Joseph P. Lash, *Roosevelt and Churchill, 1939–1941*. New York: Norton, 1976, p. 488.

81. "Tragedy at Honolulu," *Time*, December 15, 1941, p. 19.

82. Quoted in Grace Tully, *F.D.R.: My Boss*, p. 256.

83. Franklin Roosevelt's speech to Congress on December 8, 1941. Pearl Harbor.org. www.pearlharbor.org/speech-fdr-infamy-1941.asp.

84. Quoted in James MacGregor Burns, *Roosevelt: The Soldier of Freedom*. New York: Harcourt Brace Jovanovich, 1970, p. 172.

85. Quoted in Don DeNevi, *The West Coast Goes to War*, p. 56.

86. Hailey, *Pacific Battle Line*, p. 13.

For More Information

Books

Thomas B. Allen and Robert D. Ballard. *Remember Pearl Harbor: Japanese and American Survivors Tell Their Stories.* Des Moines, IA: National Geographic Society, 2001. The authors convey the human element in battle by telling the story of Pearl Harbor through the recollections of men and women who experienced it. Allen and Ballard provide a helpful overview of the attack.

Eugene Burns. *Then There Was One.* New York: Harcourt, Brace, 1944. Burns, a veteran Associated Press war correspondent covering the Pacific, gives the reader the viewpoint from the crew of the aircraft carrier USS *Enterprise*, which was steaming toward Pearl Harbor when the attack began.

Robert Casey. *Torpedo Junction: With the Pacific Fleet from Pearl Harbor to Midway.* New York: Bobbs-Merrill, 1942. Casey's book is the best available source for understanding the uncertainty and fear that existed in Hawaii in the aftermath of December 7. This is a very powerful book about the war.

Don DeNevi. *The West Coast Goes to War, 1941–1942.* Missoula, MT: Pictorial Histories, 1998. DeNevi tells the story of the war's first day and its immediate aftermath as citizens living along the West Coast experienced it. He shows how real was the fear of Japanese invasion at that time.

Joan Zuber Earle. *The Children of Battleship Row.* Muskegon, MI: RDR Books, 2001. Earle examines the attack on Pearl Harbor from the vantage point of how the event affected children and teens at the time. She produces a valuable source of information.

Charles Bracelen Flood. *Hitler: The Path to Power.* Boston: Houghton Mifflin, 1989. Flood has produced a readable, interesting biography of the German leader.

Foster Hailey. *Pacific Battle Line.* New York: Macmillan, 1944. Hailey, one of the most respected war correspondents of his time, delivers a solid summary of the war in the Pacific as it unfolded through 1944. The main advantage in turning to a book written during the war is that the reader gains a sense of how the nation viewed the war as it happened, what people felt, and how they reacted to events as they occurred.

William F. Halsey and J. Bryan III. *Admiral Halseyís Story.* New York: McGraw-Hill, 1947. This autobiography from one of the Pacific War's most acclaimed admirals lets the reader know what December 1941 was like for members of the U.S. Navy who were at sea at the time of the attack.

Wilbur D. Jones Jr. and Carroll Robbins Jones. *Hawaii Goes to War*. Shippensburg, PA: White Mane Books, 2001. Based upon the photographs and memories of relatives, the authors provide a powerful summary of Hawaii during the war. Their material covering the attack on Pearl Harbor and the immediate aftermath is especially moving.

Joseph P. Lash. *Roosevelt and Churchill, 1939–1941*. New York: Norton, 1976. Lash's book tells the story of the events leading to war through the eyes of the two most powerful leaders.

Walter Lord. *Day of Infamy*. New York: Henry Holt, 1957. Lord produced the first superb account of the war's opening action. Heavily based on survivors' accounts, the book casts light on the incredible heroics of the young men caught by the surprise attack.

Samuel Eliot Morison. *History of the United States Naval Operations in World War II*. Vol 1: *The Rising Sun in the Pacific, 1931–April 1942*. Boston: Little, Brown, 1965. Long rцegarded as one of the premier historians of World War II, Morison presents the march to war in a lively, entertaining style. This book is probably the best place to start any research into Pearl Harbor.

Ronald H. Spector. *Eagle Against the Sun*. New York: Free Press, 1985. One of the most respected historians of World War II, Spector delivers an excellent history of the Pacific War. His chapters on events leading to Pearl Harbor are especially illuminating.

Edward P. Stafford. *The Big E: The Story of the USS* Enterprise. New York: Random House, 1962. This is one of the finest books to portray life at sea for World War II sailors, not only during the December attack but also through the entire war.

Paul Stilwell, ed. *Air Raid: Pearl Harbor!* Annapolis, MD: Naval Institute Press, 1981. This superb book contains the recollections of people— diplomats, military personnel, and civilians—who experienced the events leading to war or the attack at Pearl Harbor. This valuable collection provides a compelling glimpse of a tumultuous day.

Shelley Tanaka and David Craig. *Attack on Pearl Harbor*. New York: Hyperion Books For Children, 2001. The authors use the memories of military personnel and civilians, including teenage residents in Hawaii, to create a compelling picture of the December 7, 1941, attack. Many photos support a clearly written text.

Theodore Taylor, *Air RaidóPearl Harbor!* Fairbanks, AK: Gulliver Books, 2001. Taylor takes a more traditional approach in telling the story of December 7. He presents both the American and Japanese sides as he moves from the origins of the attack to the day itself.

John Toland. *But Not in Shame*. New York: Random House, 1961. Toland's book covers the Pacific War's first six months, a time when the United States military tried to rebound from Pearl Harbor and the American public tried to make sense out of the astonishing attack. This is a wonderful book that relies on survivors' accounts to breathe life into the narrative.

Grace Tully. *F.D.R.: My Boss*. Chicago: Peoples Book Club, 1949. As Tully was President Roosevelt's personal secretary, in this book she delivers a behind the scenes view of what occurred in December 1941. The reader understands the emotions of the time and how much the attack affected Roosevelt and other influential leaders.

Dan van der Vat. *Pearl Harbor: The Day of Infamyóan Illustrated History*. New York: Basic Books, 2001. Well-known World War II historian Dan van der Vat's text that deftly accompanies the superb paintings and diagrams that illustrate the event. He has produced an effective method of recording a memorable day.

Articles

"Battle Stations." *Time*, December 8, 1941. This article depicts the preparations for war as well as the way the nation reacted to the surprise attack at Pearl Harbor. Because it was written by people who were there, it delivers an authentic sense of how the nation felt at that time.

Emily Bazar. "Stamps Honor 4 Notable Sailors." *USA Today*, February 4, 2010. www.usatoday.com/news/military/2010-02-03-ww2heroes_N.htm. This article explains why Doris Miller, an African American sailor, deserves acclaim for his heroics on December 7, 1941.

"My Brush with Destiny: A Date with a Bombing." *American Heritage*. www.americanheritage.com/articles/magazine/ah/1991/8/1991_8_36.shtml. This website of one of the acclaimed historical publication *American Heritage* contains two valuable articles from people who witnessed the Pearl Harbor attack. Stephen Bower Young recalled his time aboard the USS *Oklahoma*, while Betty Garrett viewed events from a civilian vantage.

Richard B. Frank. "Zero Hour on Niihau." *World War II*, July 2009. This article details the fascinating story of a Japanese pilot who landed his damaged aircraft on the island of Niihau, northwest of Oahu. When a handful of citizens of Japanese ancestry aided the pilot, their actions helped to provoke a mass evacuation of Japanese Americans on the mainland.

"Interview with Pearl Harbor Eyewitnesses." *Scholastic*. http://teacher.scholastic.com/pearl/transcript.htm. This website contains a revealing interview with Navy officer Hubert Dale Gano and his wife, Johnie. The couple, who resided in Hawaii at the time of the attack, shared their memories with one of the nation's premier student magazines in a feature titled, "Interview with Eyewitnesses Johnie and Dale Gano," from December 1996.

"Tragedy at Honolulu." *Time*, December 15, 1941. This article conveys the emotions and experiences of people in Hawaii at the time of the attack.

U.S. Navy. "Overview of the Pearl Harbor Attack, 7 December 1941." www.history.navy.mil/faqs/faq66-1.htm. The reports, gathered by the Naval Historical Center in Washington, D.C., provide a helpful official chronology for the different ships in the harbor.

Websites

Pearl Harbor Remembered (http://my.execpc.com/~dschaaf/mainmenu.html). This excellent site contains the experiences of seventeen individuals who participated in the December 7 attack. The various reminiscences deliver a stirring, personal account of what happened on that first day of war. Included are the stories of: Paul Urdzik, George Phraner, John McGoran, Art Wells.

Pearl Harbor.org (www.pearlharbor.org/speech-fdr-infamy-1941.asp). Franklin D. Roosevelt's speech to the U.S. Congress on December 8, 1941. Roosevelt's speech and other material relating to it can be found at this website.

Index

Picture Credits

Cover: © Bettmann/Corbis
AP Images, 6, 38, 44, 46, 49, 66, 86
© Bettmann/Corbis, 11, 27, 30, 33, 57, 69, 72, 77, 82, 92
© Corbis, 7, 25, 29, 32, 50, 55, 59, 61, 64, 94
Getty Images, 6, 75

© Hulton Deutsch Collection/Corbis, 21
© INTERFOTO/Alamy, 19, 34
The Library of Congress, 14
Photo Researchers, 9
Public Domain, 17
Time & Life Pictures/Getty Images, 42

About the Author

John F. Wukovits is a retired junior high school teacher and writer from Trenton, Michigan, who specializes in history and biography. Besides biographies of Anne Frank, Booker T. Washington, Michael J. Fox, Eli Manning, and Martin Luther King Jr. for Lucent Books, he has written biographies of the World War II commander Admiral Clifton Sprague, Barry Sanders, Tim Allen, Jack Nicklaus, Vince Lombardi, and Wyatt Earp. He is also the author of many books about World War II, including the July 2003 book, *Pacific Alamo: The Battle for Wake Island*, the August 2006 *One Square Mile of Hell: The Battle for Tarawa*, and the November 2006 *Eisenhower: A Biography*. A graduate of the University of Notre Dame, Wukovits is the father of three daughters—Amy, Julie, and Karen—and the grandfather of Matthew, Megan, Emma, and Kaitlyn.